THE
TEN
COMMANDMENTS
OF
MINDPOWER
GOLF

THE
TEN
COMMANDMENTS
OF
MINDPOWER
GOLF

NO-NONSENSE STRATEGIES FOR MASTERING YOUR MENTAL GAME

ROBERT K. WINTERS, Ph.D.

McGraw·Hill

New York   Chicago   San Francisco   Lisbon   London   Madrid   Mexico City
Milan   New Delhi   San Juan   Seoul   Singapore   Sydney   Toronto

1 2 3 4 5 6 7 8 9 0   AGM/AGM   3 2 1 0 9 8 7 6 5 4

ISBN 0-07-143479-8

This book is printed on acid-free paper.

This book was inspired by my wife, April Jeanine Winters. She has always maintained a strong belief that what you really want in life is yours for the making if you work hard to achieve it. I dedicate the ideas and strategies in these pages to all golfers who share her zeal for success and personal accomplishment.

Contents

Foreword • ix

Preface • xi

Acknowledgments • xv

Introduction • xvii

Commandment 1
Thou Shalt Have a Great Attitude • 1

Commandment 2
Thou Shalt Always Believe in Thyself • 13

Commandment 3
Thou Shalt Play Thine Own Game • 25

Commandment 4
Thou Shalt Play One Shot at a Time • 35

Commandment 5
Thou Shalt Play with Patience • 43

Commandment 6
Thou Shalt Commit to Every Shot • 51

Commandment 7
Thou Shalt Keep Thy Game Simple • 61

Commandment 8
Thou Shalt Play with No Expectations • 71

Commandment 9
Thou Shalt Play with Trust • 79

Commandment 10
Thou Shalt Never, Ever Give Up • 89

The Short Version
The Ten Commandments of Mindpower Golf • 101

Index • 103

Foreword

How often have you heard that "the game of golf is all between the ears," or that a golfer "has a good head for the game," or that a player "is a mental case"? Without question, golf is a mental game, and to play well requires concentrating, focusing, relaxing, having the will to win, controlling your nerves and emotions, being in the present moment, coping with pressure, being confident, and many other qualities. Having taught some of the world's great players through the years, I firmly believe that they have been successful largely because they won the battle within themselves and mastered the mental game. Certainly, having good technique and understanding one's own mechanics is vital and is a foundation for focused professionals. There is a tremendous depth of talent in today's golf game, but what separates the good from the great is that all-important organ between the ears.

A strong mental game is a crucial ingredient of success for golfers at every level. Even recreational players will benefit from understanding how their thoughts affect their game. Being realistic, knowing your capabilities, thinking clearly, and enjoying the game all contribute to playing better golf and shooting lower scores. Some golfers seem to have been born with a good temperament to play this demanding game; others have to learn the art of thinking well.

Whether you feel you are mentally strong or weak, *The Ten Commandments of Mindpower Golf* will help you play and score better. I have known sport psychologist Dr. Robert Winters, or "Dr. Bob," as he is affectionately known, for quite a few years. His concise message on how to apply oneself mentally in playing the game and how to improve oneself has helped an enormous number of players of all levels. Dr. Bob is the resident sport psychologist for my David Leadbetter World Teaching Headquarters in Orlando, Florida, and he has made a huge difference in our program. Whether young or old, seasoned professionals or avid weekend golfers, all who have attended my academy have benefited from his simple approach to thinking great thoughts and transferring that mental focus to the golf course—and now, so can you. You will begin to look at the game differently as you apply Dr. Robert Winters's ten commandments of mindpower golf. The game will become enjoyable instead of frustrating, easy rather than difficult. This book will help you to reach your potential. And who knows? The benefits may go far beyond just golf.

Enjoy the read.

—David Leadbetter

Hall of Fame golfer Ben Hogan once remarked that golf is 100 percent mental and 100 percent physical, and the two factions of golf cannot and should not be separated. I agree. By its very nature, golf is both physical *and* mental. It also has a strong emotional component that makes it the toughest and greatest game ever created. On the professional golf tours, what separates winning golfers is the strength of their mental game and emotional resiliency. This is why a growing number of amateur and professional players have been seeking the assistance of sport psychologists and mental coaches to help them develop mental toughness.

A number of books have offered information about the mental game in the past few years. Sadly, a number of these books are filled with complicated psychological theories or vague references to how a certain touring professional would react in a given situation. After golfers read the material, they are often confused about how to use the information. Even though these books may offer sound philosophical and psychological viewpoints, many golfers miss the message and are left asking, How does this information apply to *me*? How do I apply this information specifically to *my* game?

The Ten Commandments of Mindpower Golf is about the mental and emotional side of golf—more to the point, about *your* thoughts and emotions when you play golf. The book offers useful information about the mental and emotional game of golf and tells you specifically how to achieve a great mind-set *and* moodset today. It also details the ten most important yet misunderstood and poorly explained aspects of the mental game of golf.

I've compiled ten basic strategies that will help you improve your focus and attitude on (and off) the golf course. I have purposely used "the ten commandments" in the title to illustrate the importance of the message for your golf performance. The "commandments" are action plans for success that I have compiled throughout my years of working with touring professionals, top amateurs, collegiate players, and junior golfers.

By following the "ten commandments" and adhering to the lessons presented in this book, you can show up at the golf course armed with a clear understanding of how to plan your strategy and to think effectively. But, more important, you will create an emotional and mental toughness that will help you shoot lower scores and experience more enjoyment on the course.

I have kept the text simple and easy to follow. You can go to any page in the book and find great information right away. You do not have to start at the first chapter and read from start to finish. I have created the book to be read from any starting point or chapter that you feel will help you the most. Each chapter has a feature called "Mind Stuff: Things to Do to Play Great" that includes personal assignments to heighten your learning experience. I have also added a summary at the end of each chapter to review the major points within that chapter.

Think of this text as your personal workbook for mental and emotional training.

I have intentionally excluded from the text any specific chapter entitled "Thou Shalt Have Confidence." Confidence will show up naturally as a result of your investing yourself in the material and participating in the learning process. I have also not mentioned fun or enjoyment in the ten commandments. I happen to believe that setting a goal of "having fun" or "enjoying yourself" on the golf course makes trying to have fun too much like work. I have a lot more fun on the golf course when I become absorbed in the process and just have a wonderful time with my thoughts, my ball, and my target and let go of trying to create fun.

The foundation for this book came from my formative years as a young amateur golfer, collegiate player, touring professional, collegiate coach and instructor, and years of golf psychology research. My knowledge comes from my experience working with some of the best touring golfers and teaching professionals in the world, such as my good friend, teaching great David Leadbetter. But a major part of this book comes from information derived from some of the most *emotionally challenged golfers* in the world. It even comes from the multitude of golfers (just like you) who are constantly looking for simple tips for and secrets to consistently great golf. I know that once you start to read the following chapters you will find the text speaking directly to you.

I also believe that by reading this book you will discover many things about yourself that transfer to your life off the course. The ideas within will certainly challenge the way you currently think about your game and how you react to certain situations. In essence, this book will make you think about and perhaps reevaluate your priorities. By reading this text and following my simple instructions, you will increase your understanding of both yourself and your golfing talent. I wish you much enjoyment in your pursuit of golfing greatness by adhering to *The Ten Commandments of Mindpower Golf*.

Acknowledgments

I would like to thank touring professionals Rachel Teske, Justin Rose, Charles Howell III, Ian Poulter, Matthew Blackey, Tom Gillis, Bill Glasson, Nancy Scranton, Brian Gay, Tiffany Faucette, Tammie Durdin, Smriti Mehra, Arjun Atwal, and my good friend, David Leadbetter, for sharing their thoughts with me on the mental side of great golf.

A special thanks also goes to the late Arthur Meyers, who was always there for personal guidance and professional insight and whose help was invaluable in the production of this book. I shall always be grateful for his friendship and advice. I also want to thank Ed and Jonathan Moore, Jim Fuller, Tim Cooke, and Simon Cooke for their feedback on the original manuscript.

Finally, a great big nod of appreciation goes to the hundreds of professional and amateur golfers I have helped and counseled through the years. Their feedback has always been my best instruction.

Introduction

Golf is a very simple game, but too often players make it difficult by trying too hard or thinking too much or thinking about too many things at the wrong time. As a sport scientist, I believe one of the difficulties in playing great golf is that players often have too much time to hit the ball. After all, the ball is just sitting there waiting for you to hit it. The ball has no personality, no mind of its own, and no hidden agenda to sabotage you. Yet we frequently give the ball a life of its own; it becomes the enemy and we become its helpless victim.

An example of this is the golfer addressing his ball and taking a number of waggles trying to become comfortable. As time goes by and the player fidgets over the ball, one can sense the building tension and looming disaster. As the ball just sits there waiting to be hit, golfers frequently entertain random negative thoughts that sabotage their focus and relaxation. A poor swing and an undesirable result usually follow. The golfer becomes discouraged as he walks to find his ball, and the entire process starts all over again. What started out as a day of promise turns ugly because of one's lack of decisiveness and mental clarity.

Lack of focus and purpose create trouble. Tiger Woods once stated that "a golfer should never make a mental mistake because the ball is just sitting there waiting for you to hit it." This statement makes sense. In any sport where the athlete initiates the performance, time is an element that either helps or hurts. Taking the time to think the situation through and get a clear picture about what you are going to do when you step into the ball can certainly help.

However, taking *too much* time leads you to become analytical and, most likely, negative. Spending too much time over the ball introduces the chance for doubt to creep in and allows tension to take over, which in turn perpetuates the growing sense of doubt and worry. This self-doubt can create conscious overcontrolling thoughts while swinging the golf club, interfering with the automatic processes that should flow out of habits developed in your practice and repetition. It is the release of conscious thinking and trusting the automatic function of your training and practice that allows you to swing naturally.

Think back to the last time you played well. You probably didn't try hard, or maybe you didn't even try at all. You just went out and played golf. And right there is the dilemma. You intuitively know that "practice makes perfect" and you are motivated to want to do well, so you try hard to perfect your golf swing and work on your mental game. You spend hour after hour on the practice range hitting balls and working on your shot-making technique. You devote many of your nights to reading the latest golf strategy tips that your favorite guru has written. Now, armed with all of this information, you feel that you're ready to go to the course and break all of your personal scoring records. Before you know it, you find yourself out on the course tied up in knots trying to hit the ball "just right" and looking for the "zone." Alas, try as you might, you become paralyzed by too much thinking and are victimized by poor results.

By trying so hard to play at a proficient level, you forget the most basic ingredient for great golf, which is to just go out and play. Imagine how good you would be if you could get your mind to be childlike and innocent. Your mind would be clear. You would have no fear, no worry, no sense of the consequences that lay ahead. You would be able to forget about everything that could go wrong and swing to your target with trust. In a very real sense, you would be much better off to think this way. But in order to play better golf, you listen to your adult, logical, conscious mind that says to continue to diligently work away and search for the "answer." What you find is that there are a lot of different ideas about what to do and whom to listen to. You end up going round and round in instructional circles, only to become frustrated and confused. You exert a lot of energy and end up where you started, discouraged and still searching for a swing that works and a mind that allows you to play to your talent.

In my work with golfers of all talent levels and abilities, a primary key to achieving a positive and focused mindset has been for the player to adopt a mental and emotional action plan that helps to improve attitude and concentration while on the golf course. (And performance is the name of the game in golf.) A mental action plan can provide you with a foundation for good thinking and decision making. Making clear decisions increases your confidence and helps to remove doubt. By removing doubt, you help to eliminate worry and fear and you can swing to your target with trust and confidence. Also, thinking and acting with a focused mindset allows you to stay patient and composed even when the bounces don't go your way.

The information in this book will definitely help you learn the ultimate performing mindset. By adhering to the instructions and philosophies I describe, you will expand your playing awareness and create an understanding that provides you with a winning mindset and moodset. You will start to think with greater clarity and conviction, which leads to more decisive and purposeful movement. In a sense, you will start to play with a childlike confidence that is not tainted with doubt, indecision, or lack of trust. You will finally be able to play with emotional and psychological freedom. So, if you're ready, let's get started and create a more effective way to think and feel great about yourself and your golf game.

THE
TEN
COMMANDMENTS
OF
MINDPOWER
GOLF

Thou Shalt Have a Great Attitude

Everything in golf, and I mean *everything*, starts with your creating, nurturing, and maintaining a positive attitude for success. I like what popular psychologist Dr. Phil McGraw says when he is talking about understanding a subject or a lesson point. Dr. Phil tells his audience, "Either you get it or you don't." This remark applies directly to the importance of building a great golfing attitude. Either you "get" the idea that attitude is a vital element of your game or you don't. It's just that simple.

The problem with "you get it or you don't" for many players may stem from the notion that a great attitude is an intangible thing that can't really be measured. It's true that attitude is a psychological-emotional component that can't be measured on a stat sheet or played back on a video camera. However, when a player has a great attitude, you can sense it in the way she walks, talks, and acts on the golf course. A golfer with a great attitude stands out without having to say a word about her performance. Every player, coach, and spectator can spot a player who has a great attitude just by the way that golfer handles herself. A golfer with a poor or negative attitude also stands out, sometimes even more dramatically, by the way she talks and behaves. The following story of a young touring professional provides an excellent illustration of the power of one's attitude.

Daniel: Case Study in Attitude Adjustment

Recently a young professional golfer sought my help to figure out his lack of success on Tour. Let's call him Daniel. Daniel felt that he had all of the required tools to be a top player, but he couldn't quite understand why he wasn't successful. After all, he was one of the longest hitters on the PGA Tour and perhaps one of the finest ball strikers. Daniel remarked to me, "I just don't get what makes some of the other guys shoot lower scores than me. I've thought about this for a long time now. I've compared my skills to theirs, and mechanically, I hit the ball with more authority, I'm longer than almost everyone out here, and I sure look a lot more professional than most of them." He went on to say, "I just can't understand why they are beating me."

After listening to him explain his dilemma in further detail, my response to Daniel was simple. I told him that he was absolutely correct in his assessment of the situation. Appearing stunned, he asked me what that meant. I explained that he was correct in that he "just didn't get it" and that he would never "get it" if he didn't learn to take a look at his own attitude. This young player was so busy telling other players how good he was (when he wasn't scoring all that well) that he was burning bridges with his ego-protecting behavior. No one wants to play with someone who thinks he is better than everyone else. What does that say about your game as a playing companion or partner?

Second, Daniel was so fixated on comparing himself to other players in terms of golf swing and ball-striking ability that he became resentful of their success. He couldn't believe that other players were beating him with "inferior skills." He was also becoming deeply frustrated by his own inability to discover what component was holding him back from beating many of these other players. He was looking for an answer that was literally staring him right in the face every morning when he shaved. The problem for Daniel was that he could never see it.

Daniel, like so many golfers I talk with (at every level of the game), was making the same mental and attitudinal mistakes repeatedly and never learning from those mistakes. He forgot that the idea in golf is to get the ball into the hole in the fewest number of strokes, not to be concerned with what it looks like or what others may think. His attitude about himself and his golf game was misdirected and distorted. He became overly concerned with how he appeared to other players. He resented feeling inadequate compared to players whose skills he felt were inferior. It was unimaginable to him that they could possibly be beating him and shooting lower scores. His ego was shattered, which made him resort to a defensive mental posture that affected his ability to focus on his game and play with a sense of confidence. Daniel became bitter and reacted to his lack of success with a negative attitude that caused him to appear arrogant. This served to separate him from the other players, and that made for a lonely existence on the Tour.

I went on to explain to Daniel that the golfers who were succeeding didn't care about how far he could hit the ball or about the efficiency of his golf swing. Each one cared only about playing his own game and learning to create a personal playing attitude for his own success; he cared about how his own thoughts and attitudes affected his play, and not Daniel's. I told him that this was not a selfish attitude but a self-full one, meaning that each player is full of himself in a positive and nurturing way. Each golfer is ultimately responsible for giving himself a positive self-direction for peak performance. Each player needs to develop an attitude and mindset that he believes in his talent unconditionally. An unconditionally positive attitude is where players need to start in seeking success because it is the foundation from which all dreams are created and realized.

My prescription for Daniel was to learn that attitude is about making a choice. You can either choose an attitude that works for you or you can choose an attitude that will always work against you. What you choose to think ultimately shows up in either positive or negative golfing results.

After I had made these observations and stated my case, Daniel finally looked at me and said that he needed to take a closer look at himself and change his attitude. He realized that he needed to let go of his judgmental thoughts about other players and work on his own attitude.

Now Daniel is getting to a point where he values having an attitude that helps him stay emotionally strong and allows him to play his game versus trying to appear superior to others. Daniel now "gets it" and is able to play with a great attitude that gives him what he really needs without being sidetracked by distractions. What Daniel learned from all of this is that even if you have the sweetest swing in the world, a bad attitude will stop success in its tracks.

Attitude Is an Emotional Fuel

If you start your golfing day with a poor attitude and cannot find anything positive to draw from your round and your talent, you will never be the player that you aspire to be. Attitude is like emotional fuel. The type of fuel you use determines how far and how fast you will go. If you put cheap fuel in your car's gas tank, your car will eventually start to spurt and shut down quickly. Although cheap gas may be all right in the beginning, it is destructive to your car's well-being in the long run. On the golf course, if you fail to believe in yourself, if you talk to yourself in a harsh manner, if you beat up on yourself, you are likely to give up and become discouraged. Your ability to hang in there and put up a decent score is ruined from the start. Your "cheap gas" attitude will become a liability to your golf performance.

However, if you use premium gas in your car, you have given yourself the best fuel available to run long and smooth. In the same way, with a great "premium" attitude you can endure the shots that go astray and the putts that don't go in because you have the ability to stay focused and upbeat. If you focus on being positive and patient you will ultimately see the results on your scorecard. It's all because of your attitude. To put it another way, if you place bad thoughts and feelings in your mind, you're likely to suffer a mental collapse and call it quits. Have good thoughts and feelings in your mind and you are off to a good day. It's just that simple.

Specifically, you need to start your round with a positive attitude and expect that good things will happen. And you need to maintain an attitude that provides positive momentum for the duration of the round. Finally, you need to have a resilient attitude that allows you to accept your bad breaks and generate an appropriate and enthusiastic physical response for your next shot.

Overall, attitude is perhaps the most important club in your bag because it ultimately determines your talent and aspiration level. Your attitude is directly linked to your motivational interest in yourself. A majority of players I work with realize the importance of attitude and try to start their rounds with a positive mindset, but some are not sure how to create an attitude that will endure throughout an entire round. That is where I come in and offer some specific strategies for their review. The following section will help you create a great attitude for playing your best golf.

Mind Stuff: Things to Do to Play Great
Five Strategies to Develop a Great Attitude

The following strategies will help you create and adhere to a great attitude on the course. By adding these strategies to your golfing arsenal, you will be armed with a purposeful action plan.

Develop the "I Can Handle It" Attitude

Can you imagine yourself being able to deal with tough situations with grace and composure? If you can't, then get ready to learn this valuable technique. The next time you play and are faced with a tough shot or situation, instead of worrying about the negative consequences simply say to yourself, *I can handle it*. The power of these four words will lead you to take positive action steps. As you are pondering your shot, instead of reacting angrily to the bad lie or the anxiety of the moment, tell yourself, *I can handle this* and walk as if you have been through this tough environment many times before. Verbally tell yourself, *I can handle this situation, and I will be successful*.

Research from the field of behavioral psychology suggests that if we behave in a manner that promotes confidence, such as walking and talking with self-assurance, our feelings and thoughts will start to emulate that behavior. Therefore, if you start to act as if you can handle the situation and move in an assured fashion, you are creating a psycho-physiological pathway to composure and purposefulness. By acting confident, you will start to feel and think confidently. In this way, you take control of the situation instead of allowing the situation to take control of you.

Find the most logical and objective way to deal with the circumstances in front of you. Think through the situation thoroughly and then (and only then) make a decision about how to play the shot. The old adage "Keep a cool head while everyone around you is losing theirs" is a great one. It should be a helpful reminder to you that taking your time to let things cool down is a good strategy as well. Don't rush from making a mistake only to jump into the next shot and make another.

Remember, great golf is not easily acquired and is earned through your efforts and toil. Become friendly with tough situations. Enjoy the difficult lies and the long holes. Enjoy all types of unfamiliar situations knowing that once you face your greatest fears, they will start to dissolve. By dealing effectively with all kinds of difficulties, you will have developed a foundation that says, "Bring it on—I can handle this." As former First Lady Eleanor Roosevelt once said, "We must do the thing we fear." By facing your fears head-on and armed with an action plan, you can defeat the uncertainties of competition and outcomes. When you adopt the philosophy of *I can handle it*, you can deal with anything that comes along with poise and composure. The residue that remains from being successful in handling tough situations is known in the performance arena as *confidence*.

Win the Attitude Championship Before You Play

This idea comes from a wonderful book by noted golf instructor Jim Flick. In his book *Jim Flick on Golf*, Jim described one of his students as having a great mindset and attitude. He said that this player went into every round and every tournament knowing that he was going to win the attitude championship. Nothing or no one could keep him from succeeding at this championship. For him, the championship was about attitude, not score. What this golfer committed himself to doing was making sure that he was the most committed golfer he could be and keeping his mind and thoughts going in a positive direction. By doing this he knew that he might not always win the scoring championship, but he could give himself the best chance for success by always having his head in the right place.

I think this is a wonderful example for all of us to follow. Just think of how good you could be if you committed yourself to being as positive as you can be for an entire round instead of beating yourself up with negativity. The results would surprise you.

So the next time you play, before you enter the clubhouse gates dedicate yourself to winning your personal attitude championship. Be the most positive and resilient player in the tournament or your playing group. If you can do that, you will be well on your way to playing better golf and shooting lower scores.

Give Yourself a Pep Talk Before You Go to the Course

Just as big corporations have sales and motivational meetings, so should you. When you drive to the golf course and before you enter the clubhouse gates, remind yourself that today is your day and that your number-one goal is to stay positive throughout the round. Use positive words to stay focused. Be kind to yourself on the golf course and remain patient. Remember, it's all right to feel good about your game when things are going well, but it's even more important to feel good about your game when things aren't going well. When failure or poor play occurs, the name of the game is to improve and get better at handling these tough situations.

You can aid your performance on the course by giving yourself a pick-me-up speech at the end of a poor shot or poor play on a hole. Accept the possibility that you can turn things around by merely keeping your attitude going in a positive direction. Facing challenges head-on and hanging in there are great ways to develop mental toughness, which will enable you to reap benefits down the road. Always remember that you create your attitude and you wear it like a badge—but you have to earn that badge on every shot during your round.

Imitate a Player with a Great Attitude

They say that imitation is the sincerest form of flattery, and imitation in golf is no exception. Just as you could copy a top player whose swing you admire, you could also identify a player who has a great attitude and emulate her mindset and moodset. A good role model for you would be someone you have observed closely either by watching her on TV or by playing with her or following her in person. This player could be a professional or amateur. It could even be one of your golfing companions in your Saturday foursome.

Make a list (or mental note) of the qualities that you admire about this player and especially the way he handles himself in tough situations. For example, you may want to list how he approaches every shot with enthusiasm or his overall personality or attitude. It could be any number of things. What is most important about this strategy is that you learn how to emulate and imitate a good attitude by observing and learning from a role model. By imitating your model's good attitude and behaviors, you will be forming good habits for your own playing personality.

Define Your Great Attitude

The final strategy for building a great attitude involves a bit of thinking and doing on your part. Sit down and write out what you think are the most important qualities a golfer can have for building a great attitude. You may be surprised at what you write down. This is a serious exercise, but it is not a test. There are no right or wrong answers, just your responses and feelings. Write down what you feel is essential to creating a good attitude and then incorporate those good feelings into how you think, feel, and play. I will list a few examples to get you started.

1. *I will stay patient on the course.* A golfer with a great attitude is patient and enjoys each day on the course, regardless of the final score.
2. *I will stay resilient and composed.* A golfer with a great attitude is resilient and can stay composed through the tough stretches of a golf round.
3. *I will enjoy the process of playing golf.* A golfer with a great attitude enjoys the process of playing her best golf and looks forward to each new shot with enthusiasm and vigor.

OK, there you have it. These are just a few of the things that I try to remember when I play. They are also the qualities I look for when I observe players with good golf attitudes. You can make your list with more or less items, but the important thing is that once you identify these components, you embrace them and make them a part of your overall golfing profile.

Summary

Great golf begins and ends with your creating and maintaining a great attitude, period. Nothing is more important for your success than to adopt a great attitude starting today; but it is also the most difficult element for golfers to understand and to achieve. A great attitude may not cure your slice or eliminate your hook, but it will give you the best opportunity to see how good you can become with your physical game.

The greatest players of today fine-tune not only their swings but their attitudes. It's true that Ernie Els, Tiger Woods, and Charles Howell III all have fantastic athletic ability and have learned to develop their God-given talent. But what is more important is that they all have great attitudes that allow their talent to thrive and flourish. You may or may not have the athletic ability of these wonderful players, but you do have the same opportunity to develop and achieve a great attitude and to use it to your advantage on the golf course. Start today by tapping into your heart and mind. Once you arm yourself with a great attitude, you are well on your way to realizing your dreams of golfing success.

Thou Shalt Always Believe in Thyself

One of the toughest things to understand about golf is that it is a relatively easy game when you're playing well. Everything seems to be on autopilot. You don't have to think hard about how to swing the club—if you even have to think at all. Your images are clear and your decisions firm. You swing and the ball flies straight to your target. Intuitively, you know that you are "on." You think, *Today is my day.* Your enthusiasm is high and you silently know that you have "it."

But when you don't have "it," you desperately search for "it." Every swing is a forced effort to hit the ball squarely. The game becomes frustrating and difficult. Your thoughts are random and scattered. The lack of precision and consistency creates doubt and your mind runs wild with negative anxiety. You think, *Today is not my day.* Enthusiasm and motivation are critically low and you silently wonder, *When will I get "it"? Will "it" ever show up?*

What is this "it" that I keep referring to? "It" is a simple yet vital ingredient of success: believing in yourself. What you think about yourself is what you are and determines what you will become. Believing in yourself is a combination of positive thoughts, great attitude, and intestinal fortitude that leads you to value your true golfing self. It is the conscious and subconscious "knowing" that you can become whatever you want to become.

Among today's top touring professionals, Tiger Woods certainly has "it." So do LPGA professional golfers Rachel Teske and Annika Sorenstam. No doubt Ben Hogan, Sam Snead, Arnold Palmer, and Jack Nicklaus all had "it." Every one of these golfing greats tapped into their creative genius and gave themselves the best chance to succeed by believing in themselves. More to the point, that belief created a psychological and emotional foundation that allowed them to play golf without the worry of the dire consequences that failure often brings.

Getting to the Point of "Knowing"

Believing in yourself suggests that you can handle the adversity and the unknowns that exist in golf. It means that you can "hang tough" and move into your next shot unscathed by the hard knocks and unfairness that the game presents. In fact, believing in yourself when the chips are down, when nothing is going well, may be the greatest ingredient for building positive momentum and turning your golf game around.

However, believing in yourself is much more than just being mentally tough or emotionally resilient in the face of failure. It is also about standing over a fifty-foot putt believing that the ball is going into the hole. (And it becomes even more important when you haven't made a putt all day.) It is about standing on the first tee box of your club championship knowing that you have prepared yourself mentally and physically and that you are going to play well. It is about believing in your practice habits and knowing that what you are practicing will result in better performance on the links.

Perhaps most important, it is about knowing that if you persevere you can make your dreams a reality, whether those dreams are about becoming the best golfer in the world, the best golfer at your home club, or the best golfer that your talent will allow. This type of belief system is what I call a *knowing quality of self-belief*. The "knowing" is important because when you believe in yourself it validates your self-confidence. It allows you to play your game without the worry of messing up or appearing inept. It also allows you to fully enjoy your talent, no matter what level you play. In short, you know, or have an internal sense, that everything will be OK because you have faith in your ability. This feeling of knowing helps you trust yourself when the moment of truth arrives and you prepare to hit the ball.

It's a funny thing about this game, but the more you play, the more you realize that the most important aspect isn't just hitting the ball solidly or possessing perfect golf mechanics. Rather, it's the emotional and mental component of "hanging in there" during the lean times and not allowing your spirit or willpower to be broken. It's also the ability to feel good about developing and improving your talent. By its very nature, playing golf tends to wear you down emotionally and creates a great deal of inner frustration and psychological disappointment. Conversely, it also provides a psychological boost and creates excitement when you hit good shots and build positive momentum.

However, you might be in a slump right now and feel that you don't have the right stuff, or that maybe you aren't as good as you once thought you were. You may even doubt your ability and feel that your game is withering. Take heed, because the following sections will provide some examples of the power of self-belief.

Tiger Woods: Self-Belief Leads to Improvement

If there is one thing that makes Tiger Woods great, it is his rock-solid belief in himself and his overwhelming desire to improve. From the time he was a little boy, he has passionately pursued his dreams every day. His short-term goal has been to become even better tomorrow than he is today. His long-term goals for excellence and athletic zeal are based on a wonderful foundation of a positive self-image, which makes the golf improvement process fun.

After he won the 1997 Masters, Tiger got together with his swing coach, Butch Harmon, and went on a journey to improve his overall golf swing. Even after this record-setting major tournament win, Tiger knew in his heart that his game wasn't where he thought it needed to be. He knew that he needed to make some long-term changes to be the absolute best in the world (or at least the best in his mind).

Was this a sane decision? Think about Tiger's situation and it may leave you shaking your head. This twenty-one-year-old who had just won the greatest tournament in the world was saying to his coach, "I need to make some changes." Anyone else probably would leave his game alone and ride the wave of good fortune, but not Tiger. Instead, he took the ultimate risk by making the decision to change his swing and revamp his entire game. Many golf experts were saying at the time, "Why fix something that isn't broken?"

Well, the simple answer is that Tiger knew he needed to change some aspects of his swing in order to have long-term success, so he made the change. It took months and months of hard work and determination before the changes generated tangible positive results, but not once did Tiger lose his focus on where he wanted to go with the changes. He knew that they would pay off in the long term, even after the news media's constantly asking him, "What's wrong?" and "When will you win again?" (And if you think the constant questioning doesn't have an impact on your confidence, think about what *you* might feel like if people were constantly asking you, "What's wrong with your game?" or "When do you think you'll get it back?" If you can magnify this feeling by about a hundred, you have some idea of the personal fortitude Tiger has.)

Believing in Yourself Is *Your* Responsibility

Tiger knew his vision and believed in it. He also trusted and believed in his swing coach, Butch Harmon, and in what they agreed to work on. Even though Coach Harmon provided the outside direction and educational support for Tiger, it was Tiger who did the day-to-day work. The contribution of Tiger's coach is a reminder of an important truth: it often helps to have someone else believe in your ability too. But the ultimate decision to do the work and believe that one is on the right track has to fall squarely and solely on the shoulders of the individual golfer.

The lesson is that if you want to make changes in your game, you must accept personal responsibility to become the player you want to be. Believing in yourself and your training regimen is part of the learning and believing process, and it all begins and ends with your making an active and conscious decision to get better.

Ryder Cup Belief

Another example of how the power of belief plays a vital part in golf is vividly displayed every two years in the pressure-filled Ryder Cup. Perhaps nowhere in the golf world are the mental and emotional strains of competition more evident than in this biannual series of matches held between United States and European golfers.

Sam Torrance, captain of the 2002 European Ryder Cup team, made a significant statement about why his team rallied in the singles competition the final day to win the Ryder Cup. Sam remarked that his team of underdogs won the competition over a strong American team (anchored by Tiger Woods and Phil Mickelson) because of their belief in the team concept and in the strength that comes from within each team member. Captain Torrance said that "out of the shadows come heroes."

He was referring to his underdog rookie players, like Pierre Fulke, Phillip Price, Niclas Fasth, and Paul McGinley.

These rookies came through on the final day of singles competition when the public and media doubted their ability to persevere during the pressure of the Ryder Cup playing against a veteran-filled American squad. The rookies knew that if they went out and believed in themselves and played their own games to the best of their ability, the pieces would fall into place. Europe, anchored by the strong play of veterans Bernhard Langer and Colin Montgomerie and fueled by the victories of the rookies, went on to defeat the United States team and regain the Ryder Cup. The power of believing in oneself was made evident on the performance field once more during this most crucial of golf competitions.

One particular player vividly demonstrated the power of believing in oneself. Phillip Price, a rookie playing in his first Ryder Cup who was ranked 119th in the world, was matched against Phil Mickelson, who was rated number 2 in the world, in the final day's singles competition. Prior to playing in his first Ryder Cup, some newsmakers and reporters asked Phillip if he was willing to step down and withdraw from playing in the Ryder Cup because of his poor ranking and mediocre play leading up to the event. Because of the importance of the Ryder Cup, Phillip questioned his character and his belief system. He admitted to having doubts and negative thoughts and said that the statements made by the media hurt his pride, his ego, and, most of all, his confidence in himself.

To his credit, Phillip Price had a chat with his sport psychologist on the morning of the singles matches on Sunday.

The advice given to him was to be strong mentally and emotionally and to play a solid match and not worry about the outcome. The key points of the strategy were for Phillip to believe in his ability and play his heart out without putting so much emphasis on the results. The morning session must have had a positive effect because Price went on to win the match 3 and 2 over Mickelson. Phillip Price proved that believing in your ability makes all the difference in the world.

Mind Stuff: Things to Do to Play Great
Create a Strong Belief System for Self-Improvement

Like your golf swing, your golf belief system is based on solid fundamentals or belief keys. If you truly want to build a foundation of self-belief, you must write down some specific items that are the keys to your thinking, feeling, and behaving while playing and practicing golf. Writing down your feelings and thoughts puts them in a tangible form and gives you a chance to think things through. So get a piece of paper and pencil and start to jot down any thoughts that come into your head as you answer these questions and ponder these statements. The sooner you do this, the better your golf game and the stronger your belief system will become.

1. What is your dream goal in golf?
2. What do you feel you can achieve with your golf game?
3. What is the greatest thing that you can realistically accomplish with your golf game this year?

4. What kind of golf improvement plan do you feel you can commit to?

5. How badly do you want to achieve your goals? Are you really willing to work hard in going after your golfing dreams? (If you aren't willing to work hard for it, you probably didn't want it very much in the first place.)

6. What are three positive aspects of your golf game? Remember these things every time you think about yourself and your golf game, and especially while laying in bed at night.

7. What are three aspects of your game that need to be strengthened? Take the time to focus on these three areas and strive to strengthen them. By committing to strengthening these weak areas, you are taking steps to becoming self-reliant and disciplined—key aspects in building a strong self-belief system.

8. What is a positive aspect of your golf game that has occurred recently? Focus on it. Build on the positive feelings and remind yourself that this is just one of the many good things that will happen if you keep focusing on where you want to go rather than on what has been going wrong or what didn't work out.

9. Do you stay committed to a practice plan or strategy for your day's round? Diligence will pay off if you stay focused on what you want to accomplish. Generate within yourself positive affirmations about staying tough and hanging in there during the round.

10. How is your self-talk before you go out and play? Is it supportive or does it create doubt? A good strategy is

to give yourself a pep talk every day about the state of your golf game. Corporations and salespeople do this every morning to ensure that the day will be a success. Make this a dominant habit. Also, before you go to bed at night (and especially before a round of golf) give yourself permission to be human. Know that you will make some mistakes, but also that you are growing in confidence and self-belief and that you are on your way to playing your best golf ever.

Summary

Totally believing in yourself (and your golfing ability) when you step into a golf shot is the best asset you can possess as a golfer. No weapon in your golfing arsenal is more important than the knowledge that you can handle any situation with confidence and that you can execute any shot with high efficiency. In fact, believing in oneself is the single greatest performance asset that any person can have. I can't think of a situation or event in life where the power of self-belief won't take you wherever it is that you want to go (and it works especially well on the golf course). It can overcome any form of negativity that exists.

I realize this concept is not new. In fact, as parents we often tell our children that they can do anything they want to do as long as they have big dreams and the desire to go after those dreams. The trouble begins about the time when our children start to grow up and become educated (and often cynical). They start to give away their personal power of believing in themselves. They do this by listening to other "experts" such as their friends and coaches for *their* thoughts and ideas. They then change their basic belief systems about what is good for them, as if these other people are the experts on them and that they have all of the answers. What happens next is that the power of negativity and frustration sets in and people lose their faith, their hope, and, in the end, the power of believing in themselves.

With this in mind, remember the children's story *The Little Engine That Could*. The little engine started its journey over the huge mountain saying, "I think I can, I think I can, I think I can," and found that little by little it was making progress. Finally it reached the top of the mountain and declared, "I knew I could, I knew I could." And it all started with the little engine holding a single thought in its mind that it might have a good chance of going over the mountain.

A single thought developed into a powerful belief that led to success that no one thought was possible. *The Little Engine That Could* is a simple story, but one that you should always remember, because its very essence is what holds promise for you and your lifelong golfing success. May you always believe in yourself and go after your golfing dreams.

Thou Shalt Play Thine Own Game

"Play your own game" is one of the most common clichés used in golf. Anyone who plays golf with any frequency has heard this advice. I have found that a number of my clients, even the most experienced golfers, aren't exactly sure what "play your game" means. To them, it seems to be just a lot of talk without any relevance to their performance. But finding out how you really play *your* best is the secret to playing consistently great golf.

An example that helps to illustrate the confusion about playing your own game is when a group of golfers talks to you about *your* game. They may mention another player and say things to you like, "Now, Bob, I want you to watch what Joe is doing, because he's really got the correct technique down" or "Bob, you should be imitating Joe because he has found the secret to gaining distance." As you try to imitate what Joe is doing, you find that Joe's swing isn't anything like yours and that you have trouble trying to play Joe's tempo, rhythm, or even style of play. In reality, trying to play like Joe screws you up.

Eventually you realize that you cannot play anyone else's game, nor can they play yours. You are a unique human being with special talents and gifts. These gifts are your playing personality, which you and you alone possess. Your golf game is yours. In a very real sense, you are the proud (or not so proud) owner of your golfing talent. What you choose to do with that talent is the focus of this chapter.

The first step to being a proud owner of your golf game is to learn how to play your game the way that you have always dreamed of playing. A main goal of mine when helping golfers find their own game is to help them determine their strengths and weaknesses and learn how they can develop their golfing talent. Let me expand this concept.

You Are Your Game

Essentially, playing your game means that you play golf the only way you know how to play. It is *your way*. Your game is as individual as your fingerprints. Playing your game means that *only you* can pull off certain shots the way you perceive them. This is because *only you* can see a shot in your mind's eye, create it, and internally "know" whether this shot fits your capabilities at that particular moment. It means you can play only with what you presently possess.

Your golf game is based on your experience, style of play, attitude, physical and emotional characteristics, power, touch, and finesse. Playing your game requires your unique combination of strengths. When you are playing with someone else, you cannot control their ball or results, just as they cannot control yours. This is why during a tournament or a critical golf shot, you have to listen to your own "inner voice" instead of listening to someone else's good advice. I like what psychologist and spiritual mentor Dr. Wayne Dyer says when he speaks of being your own counsel: "You must heed the advice of your own voice and disregard the good intentions of others." Applied to golf, the lesson is that you must go with the shot (and style of play) that you think and feel is right for you, even if others give you a differing opinion. Then, when you achieve or do not achieve your results, there is no one else to praise (or blame) but you.

Playing your own game will elevate your golf experience to a new level. You will reach this new level when you do not allow yourself to become confused or distracted by others. You must discipline yourself to focus only on your game and understand what you can and cannot control.

Play to Your Golf Characteristics

Playing your game also means playing to your personality and your psychological and physical characteristics. For example, say you are short and straight off the tee with your driver but you hit your short irons well. Your strategy on a long par-five hole may be totally different from that of a power hitter. Your strategy is based on accuracy and precision. By moving the ball down the middle of the fairway, you give yourself the opportunity to put a short iron in your hands for an approach shot that will get the ball close to the pin for a possible birdie. Conversely, if you are a power player, your strategy may be to hit the ball as close to the green as you can in two mighty blows. Another option if you are a power player would be to hit a long iron off the tee on a tight driving hole, using an approach that is not too aggressive yet will still put you in a position to score well.

An endless number of variations exist for every hole; no one way is right or wrong. This is why players of all shapes, sizes, and ability levels enjoy golf. The freedom to change strategy and adapt to the course conditions is based on your judgment of your playing characteristics at any given moment. Therefore, knowing how to play your game the way that you need to play at any particular moment is vital.

Hit the Right Shot

One of the more difficult aspects of playing one's game is knowing when to be aggressive and go for a target and when to lay up and use a more conservative approach. The decision is determined by your emotional, psychological, and physical skill at that moment. Only you "know" if you are making a wise choice. You need to realistically assess the risk and reward factors of a shot and know your capabilities. Are you truly able to pull off the shot? Or do you want to appear to be "bold and aggressive" and show off for your playing partners? The choice is entirely up to you. As the saying goes, "Choose wisely."

This is why the issues of trust and confidence are important. If you don't totally believe that you can pull off a shot or have the confidence to do it, then you need to select another strategy that will assure you of success or provide you with an opportunity to score more effectively. Remember that the object of playing your game is to manage your mind, emotions, and golf ball around the course in the fewest strokes. The object is not to play like Tiger Woods or Ernie Els, but to play a game that allows you to achieve the most with the talent you possess.

It would be inconsistent or inaccurate thinking (not playing your game) and poor decision making to try to pull off a "hero" shot when you do not have the physical capability to do so. I believe that most players get into trouble when they overestimate their physical ability and talent and try to make a shot that doesn't fit their shot-making ability.

It is also a mental error to try shots you have never practiced or those with unpredictable results. These are disasters waiting to happen. You will often hear players yelling after a bad shot, "Why did I try that stupid shot? There was absolutely no way that I should have hit that shot." These players have overestimated their ability levels and are *not* playing their games. They are making unforced mental errors that can be prevented by thinking situations through and making clear decisions based on realistic self-assessment of golfing ability. You should always focus on the shot that you can execute and eliminate the danger of high-risk shots that could produce results hazardous to your score and self-confidence.

How Tom Kite Improved "His Game"

Every great player has learned to maximize strengths and minimize weaknesses. Consider Tom Kite, one of golf's all-time leading money winners and greatest players and currently a threat on the Senior PGA Tour. Tom Kite has excelled at every level of the game by understanding a basic premise of golf performance: You create your edge over competitors by outthinking them and outworking them. Tom has earned the reputation as one of the hardest-working and smartest players on the Tour because he learned from a very early age that brains plus sweat equals success.

A few years ago, Tom recognized that although he was "sneaky long" he didn't have the physical capability of reaching many of the longer par-five holes in two shots and perhaps was losing a stroke per round to the longer hitters. What was he to do to give himself an edge and become more effective at making birdies on the par-five holes? The solution was to put another wedge in his bag. This allowed him to carry three wedges and become extremely accurate from 120 yards and in and play aggressively for the pins.

By virtue of thinking through the problem, Tom came up with a solution that helped him become a more proficient scorer; this, in turn, completely revolutionized the short-game wedge industry. Tom realized that putting another wedge in his bag allowed him to close the yardage gap between a pitching wedge and a regular sand wedge. This extra wedge allowed him to play with more confidence, knowing that he could get the ball close to the hole and make more birdies. Tom Kite has become one of the game's greatest players by understanding one basic rule: He plays his own game and he knows it better than anyone.

Playing Your Game at Your Speed

Playing your game also means playing at your optimum speed or overall tempo. Do not allow yourself to make hurried decisions just because you are playing with a couple of quick players. Staying within a consistent tempo and playing rhythm allows you to experience a sense of timing and flow for the entire round, which should lead to a better overall game.

On the other hand, if you are playing with extremely slow and deliberate players, do not allow yourself to become impatient with or frustrated by their pace. Keep yourself focused on what you are doing and occupy yourself by moving and staying loose. Preplay the upcoming shot in your mind and take some practice swings emulating the exact movement you intend to use.

Remember, playing your game is about enjoying *your* day and giving every shot your best effort and commitment. You do that best when you are playing at the speed and pace that allows you to stay "target focused" versus "people focused."

Mind Stuff: Things to Do to Play Great
10 Tips to Help You Play Your Game

One of the greatest joys in golf is to hit a shot that turns out just the way you imagined it in your mind's eye. This elation is one of the reasons we keep going back to the golf course, forever in search of that one great shot. However, a number of distractions may interfere with your thought process and prevent you from playing your best. Following is a list of ten tips that will help you develop and play your game. If you can commit to adopting at least four or five of these tips into your golf game for the early part of the season, you will be surprised at how much your score will improve.

1. Always play at your own pace and speed.
2. Hit your ball *only* when you are totally focused on and committed to your target.
3. Don't allow yourself to become critical and negative during the round. Always find good things about your game and keep your self-talk positive and upbeat.
4. Play with a present focus; tell yourself, *I am focused on the "now." I am focused on this moment.*
5. Do not place huge expectations on yourself for the day, the score, or the tournament. Leave the expectations at home and just play golf.
6. Avoid comparing yourself to others.
7. Plan your strategy for an upcoming shot or hole and stick to that plan.
8. Learn to stay patient and remain calm during the ups and downs in your round.
9. Don't allow yourself to be intimidated by other players. Do your own thing and do it well.
10. Don't hit a club or play a hole in a way that is incorrect for you. Play only those shots that you feel comfortable with and know that you can hit.

Summary

One of the best ways to improve your golf score is to learn how to play your own game and stay committed to your game plan. I am constantly reminding players to stick to their own game plan and to forget about anyone else or what the day's outcome may bring. The key is to stay focused on what you can control—and that is thinking, feeling, and executing your own game plan on every shot the entire day.

I like to think that playing your game is similar to what legendary crooner Frank Sinatra was singing about in the song *My Way*. This is good advice that can be applied directly to your golf game. As the song suggests, you need to be able to say to yourself after your round that "I did it my way." If you play your own game and adhere to your personal playing characteristics, you will find that your scores and your attitude will improve.

Thou Shalt Play One Shot at a Time

Has anyone ever offered you one of these tips?

- Play one shot at a time.
- Stay in the present moment.
- Don't get ahead of yourself.

Sound familiar? Many well-intentioned golfers have given these golfing tips to themselves *and* their playing partners in an effort to help them score better. For the record, these *are* good tips, but many golfers are not sure what "playing one shot at a time" means, much less how to create a one-shot mindset. In this chapter I will define one-shot mentality and explain how to develop a moment-by-moment strategy so you can score your best.

Staying in the Moment: An Exercise

Let's do a test. Look around you and familiarize yourself with your surroundings. Go ahead. Look around your environment right now. I will wait for you.

35

I would like for you right now to focus on the color blue. At this moment, I want you to look up at everything that is blue. Go ahead.

Now that you have seen how you can focus on blue, look up and focus on the bluest object that you can see. If there is no blue object, look for a green object. Focus your attention on this object for at least thirty seconds. Do not think about anything else while doing this exercise.

You have now learned how to mentally "set" your mind to a specific task by adhering to the instructions given to you via written directions. When I wanted you to look at blue, your attention was drawn to anything that had the color blue in it. You could also switch your focus to anything green. These simple visual concentration exercises you just completed demonstrate how you can visually stay in the present moment. You can do the same by listening to your inner voice when you play on the golf course. Learning how to focus on one thing is a basic step to learning how to play one shot at a time because it will help keep you in the present moment, with nowhere to go but the present shot or situation that you are focusing on *now*.

Simple Definition of the One-Shot Mindset

Simply put, playing one shot at a time means that you are focused on the shot you are currently facing and nothing else. Your awareness and focus are directed toward this shot and *only* this shot.

By focusing your attention on the shot at hand, you give yourself the best chance of success because your mind and body are totally in the present moment. Whether your current shot is your opening tee ball, an approach shot onto the green, or a putt on the eighteenth, your entire focus is on executing one shot at one particular moment and hitting it to the best of your ability. You ruin any chance of achieving a one-shot mentality when you are over your ball and thinking about such things as how many strokes you have taken on the present hole or how you missed a shot a couple of holes back or how poorly you have been hitting the ball all day. The examples that come to mind are too numerous to mention, but if you are not concentrating on the shot at hand you are probably doing one of two things that take you out of the present moment and prevent you from scoring your best. Let's explore this dilemma further.

The Present Moment's Foes: The Past and the Future

If you find it hard to concentrate on the present shot, you may be allowing your focus to drift from the shot you are currently playing and projecting your awareness into the future (upcoming shots and holes to play). Say you are getting ready to attempt a putt for a birdie on the twelfth green. As you address the ball, your mind projects forward in time to the fourteenth hole (which is a short par-five). You might be saying to yourself, "If I can make a birdie there (as well as here), then I'll be two under for the tournament." This type of thinking takes you out of the present moment and distracts your ability to properly focus your attention on what needs to be done to make your current birdie putt.

A second way that your mind works against you to take you out of the present moment is when you reflect back into the past and dredge up old memories. I am not saying that reflecting back in the past is always a bad idea, because in some instances it might be a good strategy. For example, you might think about a great shot from the past to get confidence for the present moment. However, many golfers focus only on bad-shot memories, and this type of thinking brings anger, worry, and frustration into the present moment.

Many golfers sustain the present-moment shot philosophy for a little while and then revert to their old way of thinking about their round. How can golfers learn to *stay* in the present moment and maintain a one-shot mindset? Following are some ideas that will help.

Six Steps to Staying in the Moment

It is vital to recognize that great and consistent golf is a process, not just a score or numeric result. Ultimately, this means that a golf shot is much more than just hitting the ball with your physical golf swing. Rather, it is a culmination of a series of events that leads to the hitting phase of the golf swing and encompasses the acceptance of the result. In totality, the phases of any single golf shot comprise six simple steps. Understanding these steps can guide you in developing a one-shot mind-set and staying in the moment. The steps are as follows:

1. Assessing the shot (determining the lie, wind, distance to the target, your feelings and thoughts about the shot, and other organizational data)
2. Analyzing all of your options for hitting the correct shot and processing those components with your talent and skill level
3. Making a clear and purposeful decision about what type of shot you will hit
4. Committing to the shot you have chosen and stepping into the ball with a trusting mind
5. Hitting the golf ball (the physical execution of the swing)
6. Accepting the result (whether it was productive or unproductive)

Most golfers feel that the physical portion of hitting the ball (the fifth component) is the golf shot, but that is only one small portion of the entire process. In fact, I feel that the most important part of hitting great golf shots is assessing and analyzing your options and then making a clear decision about what you are going to do before doing it. This means that for any one shot, there is a time to think and a time to act. Don't confuse your thinking with your acting.

When you stand over a shot trying to determine what you can and cannot do, consider what the present situation gives you. You first must check out the lie and other environmental factors such as wind, climate, and distance. This is the assessment phase of the shot. You also have to assess your own physical and psychological climate (your personal feelings of confidence and momentum) and factor those elements in. You then analyze all of the different options that will bring you the best chance of executing the shot effectively. This is the analysis phase. By using your mind to objectively and logically assess and analyze the situation, you have given yourself a chance to think the shot through. This process helps you to make a clear and purposeful decision about what type of shot you can hit.

Making a clear and purposeful decision is the third and perhaps the most important component of the shot-making process. Making a clear decision based on your assessment and analysis of the situation informs the hitting phase of the shot. This is because when you take the time to think a shot through (given a situation-specific thought process), you stay in the present moment and think about that one particular shot to the exclusion of any others.

The fourth component is to commit to your decision making and ready your mind and body to step into the ball and hit the shot. Committing to the shot with a purposeful mindset helps to increase your confidence and diminish doubt. It also gives your mind a mental command that says, *I am going to do this now.* Having this mental command helps to ensure that when you step into the ball you have a purposeful attitude to complete your task of hitting the ball to your target.

All that is left to do now is to initiate your preshot routine and "hit your decision." (Because the hitting phase of the golf shot is the phase where you execute your decision with a swing or putt, essentially you are merely "hitting your decision.")

The sixth and final step of the one-shot mindset is to accept your result. For most golfers, accepting the outcome is the hardest part because they base whether they are playing well (or not playing well) on the shot's result. But when you view the shot as a process rather than a result, you realize that the result is much easier to accept when you have taken the time to think the shot through and executed your decision.

Mind Stuff: Things to Do to Play Great
Take Baby Steps to One-Shot Success

A simple way to think about the one-shot mentality is to liken it to the ancient saying "A journey of a thousand miles begins with a single step." The same is true for a round of golf. Each shot along the way of an eighteen-hole round can be viewed as a series of single steps. Viewing your round in this way helps you to perform shots one at a time, one after another, with equal focus and intention. It is vital to your scoring success that you do not jump backward or forward in your mind during this "baby step" process. Staying patient and playing within yourself will help facilitate the power of staying in the present moment. The next time you play, use a baby step process. This moment-to-moment focus will help produce lower scores.

Summary

Professionals on the PGA and LPGA Tours endorse the one-shot mentality every week when you hear them state in the winner's circle, "All I wanted to do was to stay focused and patient and play one shot at a time." Many times during their rounds, players who are committed to the one-shot mentality find that they become so absorbed in the process that they forget how many holes they have played or even how well they are doing. Many low rounds have been recorded by players becoming so focused on playing one shot at a time that they forget the score and create a "flow performance state" that allows them to score lower than they ever thought possible.

Perhaps the greatest value of the one-shot mindset is that it can be applied anywhere on the golf course by golfers of all skill and talent levels. If you can assess and analyze each shot, make a clear decision about what you are going to do, commit to your decision, and then swing away with trust and accept your result, you will be well on your way to creating a mind that plays one shot at a time. May you always play in the present moment and give each shot your best effort.

Thou Shalt Play with Patience

Jack Nicklaus may have said it best when he remarked that the player who could keep his head on straight down the stretch in a major tournament was the one who was most likely to be standing after all the shots have been fired. He was referring to the value of being patient, thinking with a clear head, and, most important, staying emotionally and mentally composed.

Nicklaus stayed composed throughout his entire career. He once remarked that only one time did he ever lose composure during a heated part of a major golf competition. The proof of the wisdom of his words is in the record books: he has the greatest number of major victories as well as an incredible number of runner-up and top ten finishes. Jack Nicklaus remains golf's definitive model for ultimate patience and performance composure.

Soft Statistics

During the past few years, the PGA, Champions, Nationwide, and LPGA Tours have provided official statistics on driving, greens in regulation, putting, sand play, and many other categories that give serious golf students a remarkable way to monitor a specific player's progress. More than a dozen different scoring and ball-striking categories are available to measure one's play. I call these statistical categories *hard statistics*.

However, the categories that measure physical talent tell you nothing about two of the most important qualities of golf: patience and composure, which I refer to as *soft statistics*. Although the Tour's hard statistics don't measure these qualities, patience and composure are an essential part of a player's development and effectiveness. Every golfer who plays tournament golf (or recreational golf for "skin" money) knows this to be true. My job as a sport psychologist is to help athletes nurture their talent and find ways to be effective. A large part of that job is helping athletes to believe in themselves when things are going well, but an even more important part is to help them believe in themselves when things aren't going well.

This is an important lesson and one that the dominant player today, Tiger Woods, has learned well. Tiger discovered that in order to elevate his play, he had to commit to play his game and to believe in his talent. He raised his own standard of performance when he mastered the mental skills of not giving up, staying patient and composed, believing in himself when things were going well, and believing in himself *even more* when things were going askew. Tiger learned to monitor his performance by examining both hard and soft statistics. You should do this as well.

Tiger Woods: Staying Patient and Composed

One official PGA statistic that does indicate a player's ability to remain patient and stay on task regardless of bad shots or bad scores is called *bounce-back*. This category represents the percentage of time where a player goes over par for a hole and "bounces back" to score under par on the following hole. What the average player can learn from this category is that if you have a bad hole or score, you should emulate the best players and learn how to put the past behind you and refocus on your next shot and hole.

The ability to stay patient, remain composed, and bounce back from adversity was demonstrated impressively by Tiger Woods during the final round of the 1999 World Golf Championships. The tournament that year was held at the renowned Valderrama Golf Club in Sotogrande, Spain, which has been host to many famous golf championships. (Valderrama Golf Club has also hosted many treacherous breakdowns and caused high numbers from some of the world's greatest players due to the severity of its greens and elbowed fairways.)

On Sunday, Tiger was hitting his third shot into the long, par-five seventeenth hole with a knock-down nine iron from a distance of about 110 yards. He was hitting into a blustery direct wind toward a green that was sloped severely from the back to the front edge. Even the front approach area surrounding the front edge of the green was shaved to promote balls that were hit too short, causing these errant shots to roll back into the water.

If you had the chance to watch this event on television, you would have seen the video replay showing Tiger acknowledging the crowd's roar as the ball hit the green. As he walked up to the green and handed his club back to his caddy, he assumed he had hit a good shot past the pin to around fifteen to eighteen feet. Instead, he could only watch helplessly as he saw his ball (and his lead) roll back into the watery grave.

Nevertheless, Tiger was able to maintain his composure and continue to play his game. He hit another shot toward the hole and stayed focused on each successive shot. He eventually scored a triple-bogey 8 before proceeding on to the eighteenth tee.

We may never know for sure what Tiger was thinking as he walked from the seventeenth green to the eighteenth tee, but one thing we do know from the events that immediately followed: he dismissed the past (thoughts of knowing that he had just triple-bogeyed a hole and that it may have cost him the championship) and stayed focused on the present moment, the tee shot on the eighteenth hole.

Tiger hit his drive into the middle of the eighteenth fairway and made a par on the last hole to put himself into a position to tie Miguel Angel Jimenez for the championship and earn a place in a possible playoff (which he later won by making a birdie on the first playoff hole). Although Tiger did not score under par on the eighteenth hole during the regulation round and this would not constitute a true bounce-back statistic, what we learn from this episode is the value of patience, staying emotionally and mentally composed, and moving forward with the belief that everything will turn out OK.

Looking back at the situation, Tiger must have realized that the seventeenth hole was playing extremely difficult and that he did indeed hit a good third shot into the green. The mature and patient Tiger did not let the result upset him or wreak havoc with his confidence. Staying in the present moment and maintaining his composure allowed him to figure out what he had to do on the eighteenth tee. Staying emotionally composed allowed Tiger to assess the situation with a clear head and to believe that everything would turn out OK. This is a dramatic lesson for every golfer to learn.

Patience Is Confidence Waiting to Happen

If you have a bad hole or a bad shot, forget the score and dismiss the emotional devastation. Realize that you must clear your mind, move forward, and keep reminding yourself that your game and confidence are intact and that everything will turn out all right. It is so important that you maintain your belief in yourself and that you remind yourself that you have the talent to persevere.

Patience is confidence waiting to happen. This means that staying patient and focusing on the things that you can control while playing within yourself will allow you to play your best golf day in and day out. Also, staying patient and giving yourself the emotional space to relax and not force things to happen will keep you focused on the shot at hand instead of allowing your mind to wander to thoughts of negative shots or past high scores.

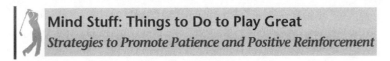

Here are three specific strategies to help you learn to be patient and to reinforce a positive view of yourself and your golf game.

Focus Your Awareness on Yourself

Any time during a round of golf or when you are waiting in line (such as at a grocery store, the movies, or a traffic light), focus your awareness on yourself and monitor your feelings. Reflect on what you are currently thinking and feeling: are you becoming bored and lethargic? Frustrated and angry? If you are a bit tense and are becoming frustrated because you hate to wait around, first acknowledge your feelings of impatience. Recognize that you are losing your focus and that you're making yourself upset. You must understand that at this particular moment you need to calm yourself. Replace your tension and anxiety with a quick and easy "mental massage."

First, inhale and take a deep breath. Hold your breath for a couple of seconds and then exhale with your mouth slightly open. As you are breathing out, think and say to yourself slowly and deliberately, *I am patient and in control*. Second, look up into the sky and allow your eyes to softly focus on any image that grabs your attention. By taking deep breaths in and out for a few seconds and using your visual focus to look up and out, you can provide yourself with a quick and easy "mental massage" that will help you become centered. If you do this mental exercise often enough, you will find that your attitude, tempo, and overall rhythm start to normalize. Performing this little verbal mantra on and off the golf course will help you to deal effectively with long waits or any sudden, unexpected events that occur during a golf round.

Swing Your Anger Away

The second strategy is to "swing your anger away." After hitting a poor shot, rather than getting angry and hastily walking to the next shot just to make another mistake, first take the time to let the dust settle and give yourself some space. Take a deep breath and let the bad thoughts go. Then take two swings and swing away any anger and frustration. This gives you the chance to release the negative results from your immediate past and helps to create a clear mindset and moodset for your next shot. This swing-away sequence is important because it creates an element of proactive venting until you are ready to move on to the next shot. It allows you to physically express your negative energy and practice your swing in order to improve it on the next shot. Take a third and final swing to reinforce the correct swing sequence you want for the next shot.

Use Positive Self-Talk

Talk to yourself in a kind and friendly manner. Use your self-talk to soothe and pacify your frustrated feelings. Always use positive words to accentuate your good play. When playing poorly, use words that are motivating and inspiring. Reward yourself verbally and mentally for "hanging in there" and being mentally and emotionally strong during a tough stretch. Give yourself a pep talk when you are feeling a bit down. Always use words to increase your confidence. Dismiss words that could be viewed as negative or could hurt your self-esteem and self-confidence. Staying focused on the task at hand and not allowing yourself to become unglued by setbacks gives you a foundation for building enduring confidence and patience on the course for the immediate future as well as for later rounds of golf.

Summary

Every top golfer knows that his or her game is going to have its ups and downs. It seems that the golfers who win the tournaments or score well are always the ones who find ways to stay calm, remain patient, and keep their composure when bad things happen or their swings are off. Patience and composure are two of the most important mental skills for short- and long-term improvement. And even if they don't show up on official year-end statistical charts, every golfer can realize the short- and long-term benefits of being patient and staying composed. May you always stay composed and have the patience to play your own game.

Thou Shalt Commit to Every Shot

Commitment. By definition, it is a pledge, a promise that something or some act will be fulfilled faithfully. When you say *commitment* or *I commit*, it is understood as a bond of action. A vivid example of commitment (outside the golf course) is found in the sacred union of marriage. The question "Do you take this man (or woman) to be your lawfully wedded spouse until death do you part" and the response "I do" are spoken aloud as proclamations of promise and trust. They are saying to themselves, to each other, and to the world that they commit to the other person in mind, body, and spirit. Couples who commit to each other in this holy matrimony and dutifully fulfill their pledges find that their lives are fulfilled, though challenged, to a purposeful end.

What has become a sad truth in our contemporary Western society, however, is that it is much simpler and easier for a person to *get* married than it is for a person to *be* married or to *stay* married. Many people find that being married and committed to another person is too much work or that their idea of commitment is not the same as that of the other spouse. People's failure to truly commit themselves often results in broken promises and failed marriages. The causes of these failures are far too complicated to discuss here, but lack of commitment in both parties is often a major factor. The same lack of commitment can also be found on the golf course.

Committing to Your Golfing Self

You may be asking, *What does all of this mean? What do commitment and pledging my faith have to do with my golf game?* Well, my fellow golfer, commitment means everything in golf. Because in golf, the commitment is not to another person, but to yourself. And when you let yourself down, you have no one to blame but yourself. That is why making the commitment to be the best player you can be must be solid from the very start. When you commit to playing great golf, it is not to be taken lightly, because commitment is a proposition and pledge to be performed dutifully until you attain your goals.

When you commit you make a promise to yourself that you are in this endeavor for the long haul and will persist until you succeed. This determined quality is a primary formula for success in any endeavor and is vital for great golf. In fact, the main difference between the top players on the professional tours and the wannabes is their commitment to a lifelong strategy of self-improvement and increasing their golfing potential.

Veteran Golfer's Story of Commitment

A few years ago, a two-time U.S. Open champion told an aspiring Tour rookie that the key to being successful in the professional golf world is not to say to yourself, *I will give myself X amount of time until I will be successful*. He told him that being a professional golfer takes time and an ultimate commitment to achieving one's dreams. He stated that even if he hadn't won his Open championship and kept his card on the PGA Tour he would still be playing on the developmental and mini-tours, simply because playing Tour golf is what he does.

This veteran and Tour winner considered himself to be a traveling professional golfer (even before he became successful) and he wasn't about to short-circuit his chances for ultimate success. He didn't give himself an ultimatum to achieve his goals or else pack it all in, because if he failed he knew that everything he had worked so hard for would be viewed as having been wasted. Instead, he chose the path of ultimate commitment. He went on to reveal that the great players at any level—junior, collegiate, amateur, and professional—must make personal sacrifices and commitments to their dreams and pursue them steadfastly. The following story illustrates the importance of commitment.

The Chicken and the Pig

While completing my doctoral work at the University of Virginia, one of my professors told a wonderful story about the importance of commitment and the implications of involvement: There once was a farmer who was going to have several important members of the county board of commissioners come to his house to inspect his farm and eat a business breakfast. The farmer went to his livestock and asked for volunteers to help with the preparation of this important meal. Two animals stepped forward, a chicken and a pig. The farmer noted to the other animals that it was quite magnanimous of these two to volunteer and thanked the chicken and the pig enthusiastically.

Upon completion of the meeting and breakfast, the farmer again went out to address his livestock and tell of the event's impact. He asked the chicken to step forward and take a bow. The farmer then told his livestock that the meeting was quite successful and that the breakfast was fabulous with ham, bacon, eggs, toast, and buttermilk. As the crowd of animals went back to the farm lot and fields something was amiss. The pig was missing from the congregation. While the chicken had volunteered her services by giving the farmer fresh eggs for the breakfast, the pig had volunteered his services by being slaughtered to give ham and bacon. The chicken was merely involved in the preparation of this meal while the pig was totally committed to the breakfast and gave his life for it.

The moral to this story is that if you really want something, you must be willing to make large sacrifices for it and not merely go through the motions to achieve it. You must be willing to totally commit to your goal, much in the same way that the pig committed to the prospect of creating the most wonderful breakfast the farmer ever had. Likewise, a large majority of golfers merely talk about wanting to play great and only involve themselves with improvement through practice. However, the players who make a total commitment to their golfing success are the ones who eventually get to the top, whether it is their club championship, their personal scoring record, or the U.S. Open. The bottom line is this: Being involved is OK, but if you want to succeed in golf and life, you must have the commitment of a pig and give it 100 percent.

Mind Stuff: Things to Do to Play Great
Strategies to Build Commitment

Strengthening your commitment for optimal preparation, practice, and golf performance is critical. If you can adhere to the following principles, your commitment level and golf progress will be bound to improve.

Commit to Your Golf Goals

In order to truly commit to becoming better, you must make an honest assessment of what is holding you back from reaching your potential. Identify what specific actions you need to take in order to address any weaknesses and make a solemn promise to yourself that you will do whatever it takes to accomplish your golf goals.

For instance, if you are having problems with your short game within forty yards of the flag (your lob-wedge game), create a specific goal to spend a certain amount of your practice time hitting lob-wedge shots. Knowing exactly what you need to work on and setting a goal to overcome that problem area is an effective way of creating a personal commitment to improvement that will yield tangible results in all areas of your game and increase your scoring potential as well.

Also, by committing to lower your handicap by a certain number of strokes in a particular time frame (for example, lower it by five strokes from the start of the spring season until the end of the fall season), you can set identifiable measures of progress and honor your commitment to those time and skill constraints. Just saying "I want to get better" is an ineffective way of framing your goals. Being specific about what you want to accomplish and then pledging to yourself that you will do these specific things in a timely fashion makes it more likely that you will see real improvement.

Commit to a Practice Schedule and Exercise/ Nutritional Program

Another way to strengthen your commitment level is to create a practice program and stick with it. Having a specific practice schedule to follow and assessing it from time to time forces you to put aside certain hours of the week to practice all aspects of your game. For instance, you might need to practice 25 percent on your long game, 25 percent on your irons or approach game, another 25 percent on your short game, and 25 percent on your putting and specialty shots, such as bunker play and trouble shots. A schedule helps you focus attention on all areas of your game, making your practice time productive and purposeful rather than random and scattered. You can alter your practice time to meet your particular schedule, but the main thing is that you commit to doing things in a structured and organized way in order to maximize the focus of your attention for that time.

Many of the top players not only have a specific physical ball-striking schedule, but they also commit to increasing their physical strength. You will find almost every top player in the world committing to some type of exercise program and special nutritional program to maximize strength and fitness. You need to develop a proper diet and exercise regimen, but remember that technology can only take you so far. If you can become stronger and more golf flexible, however, you can hit the ball longer and decrease susceptibility to injury and fatigue on the course.

Commit to Your Preshot Routine

The next time you are practicing or playing, commit to the steps that make up your preshot routine. A number of players I work with feel that they have an organized and consistent setup and routine, but they often vary it from shot to shot or hole to hole. In reality, they don't have a routine at all. In fact, the only consistency in their games is that they are inconsistent in their thoughts and behaviors every time they step up to hit the ball. This is no way to create a foundation for success. Having an established routine means that you will do the same things repeatedly in an orderly fashion and that the overall process is automatic and consistent.

One of the best ways to assess your present level of commitment is to practice committing to your preshot routine while warming up on the range. This is a form of rehearsing your commitment during your preshot ritual. Having to monitor and assess your steps consciously for a number of shots will help make you aware of going through your routine in an orderly fashion. Remember, though, that it takes a great deal of time to rehearse those separate component steps that help make your routine routine.

Remember that the time to practice your routine is not on the golf course, but on the range. Having your routine ingrained when you go to the golf course will help you perform without conscious thought. If you find yourself losing shots during a heated part of the competition, the problem probably isn't in the physical swing itself but in the inability to perform automatically. This is where your preshot routine comes in— to subconsciously assure your internal motor system that everything is going well and that you can perform automatically without having to think about the swing while standing over the ball. The benefit of committing to your routine is knowing that your swing will be automatic and that you will be able to clearly focus on your target.

Commit to the Shot and to Your Target

Perhaps the most important commitment in the game of golf is commitment to your decision making and to the type of shot you want to hit. By making a clear decision about what type of shot you want to hit, you address the ball with a specific plan for what you want to do. This purposeful action ensures that you are focused in the moment and that all you have to do at this moment is to execute your decision by hitting the shot that you have preplanned and preordered. By committing to the moment you also commit yourself to the target (where the ball needs to go). Your eyes provide the signal for where the ball needs to go, instead of focusing on something or somewhere you want to avoid. (For this reason it is vitally important to always look at your specific target and not focus on the possible hazards.)

When you start your preshot routine and step into the address position, it is a good habit to begin with a positive affirmation. This helps you focus your self-talk and stay committed to the task. Also, when stepping into the shot knowing that you are making a strong commitment to the task at hand, you can swing away to your target with confidence without the worry of negative outcomes.

Summary

At every talent level in golf, commitment is a quality that separates good golfers from poor ones. The difficulty with being committed and staying committed is that it is hard and takes a lot of work. In my work as a sport psychologist I have seen that the truly great players are the ones who honor their commitments to themselves and incorporate that commitment level into every phase of their golf games. I hope that you can attain that same inner strength to commit to your golfing moment. May you always commit to your target, and may you reach it with confidence.

Thou Shalt Keep Thy Game Simple

In his landmark instructional book *Sam Snead Teaches You His Simple Key Approach to Golf*, Sam Snead wrote (pages 4–5):

> As hard as this game is, there should be some way for more people to play it more enjoyably. . . . I want to make it as easy as possible for a person to play golf as well as possible and for as long as possible. . . . As a result, my views may sound too simple and straightforward at times, but I've never been a great believer in complicating the issue unnecessarily.

I couldn't agree more. Perhaps the great "Slammin' Sammy" knew all along that although golf is a very complex game, it is absolutely necessary to keep the objectives of the game as simple as possible. His embracing simplicity was a major reason why Sam Snead was one of golf's greatest winners and smoothest swingers. And it seems that every great player from every era in golf has commented on keeping the game as simple as possible as well.

A key characteristic in playing great golf is to understand and "know" your swing and yourself so that you can play with psychological freedom and confidence. Keeping your overall game strategy simple will help reduce your frustration of "trying harder" and make the process of playing golf seem like fun instead of work. Also, keeping your playing strategy focused on the simple task at hand will help to keep you in the present moment and allow you to play to your maximum efficiency.

Simplicity Is Success

I believe it is extremely important for all golfers to realize that keeping your golf thoughts and swing technique simple does not imply that you are stupid, inept, or unsophisticated about your game. Nor does it mean that you cannot (or do not) understand how the golf swing functions or what the important characteristics of a good swing are. What it does mean is that the golf swing and various playing aspects can be as complicated and technical as you want to make them, but they need not be made difficult. It is a good strategy to simplify your game in order to gain understanding and consistency.

As we monitor the duration and consistency of great golfers' careers, it seems that the best players are those who understand their golf swings and have fewer moving parts in which to synchronize the entire swinging motion. This implies that simplicity in approach leads to more consistency and long-term success than an overly technical or complicated approach does. Hale Irwin has maintained simplicity in form and function. His simple approach to swinging the golf club and playing his game with mental efficiency has served him well for a stellar career.

The Paper Clip: The Ultimate Device for Simplicity and Function

Think about a paper clip. Mechanically, the paper clip is just a piece of thin wire bent in such a way that when it is pushed slightly in the middle, a bit of residual tension is exhibited on the middle and outer frames of the wire. By this mechanical operation of oppositional tension, the paper clip performs a necessary function of holding and organizing important papers and letters together. I know that a lot of people who use the paper clip wonder why and how the paper clip was first invented. Many more wonder, "Why didn't I think of that?"

The key point here is that the paper clip is not fancy or highly complex. It is a great illustration of an everyday mechanism that works consistently and performs a necessary function repeatedly without breaking down. We should all be so lucky as to have our golf swings and golfing minds perform as consistently and efficiently as the simple paper clip.

How can you learn to keep things simple? Where do you start to cut out the technical fat and overthinking that interferes with your golf progress? Start right here.

Mind Stuff: Things to Do to Play Great
Tips for Keeping Your Golf Game Simple

This section is a compilation of seven mental and physical tips for playing your best golf ever. Implement these simple ideas for a thirty-day period and monitor your improvement in that period. I think you will be very surprised at your personal growth and enjoyment of the game.

Keep Your Golf Goals Simple and Specific

Keeping your golf goals simple means just what it says. Keep your goals simple enough to implement, making sure that they are also realistic and attainable. It is a wonderful goal to want to play professional golf, but if you are a 20 handicap, your immediate goal should be to lower your handicap to single digits first; then move on to lowering your handicap to scratch, and so forth. It is important that you keep your goals realistic and achievable so that you can maintain motivation to achieve those goals before you create and set new ones.

If you truly want to improve your golf proficiency, examine the areas of your golf game where you take the most strokes. Monitor your game and keep track of your problem areas and where you are losing the greatest number of shots. In this way you can discover exactly which areas you are weak in and which areas you excel in. Be specific about your goals and the time period you want to achieve your goals in. Specificity helps you to focus your attention and energy into bringing about desired actions and behaviors.

Keep Your Practice Sessions Simple

Don't waste your time practicing myriad situations that take your mind racing from one practice element to another. Golfers who start to practice one thing and jump to another before the first practice skill is learned or improved find themselves not really learning anything at all, or not improving to a high degree of proficiency and consistency. It is a good idea to have a written action plan describing what you want to practice at a given time and to stick to that plan. Many times on Tour, a player will focus on only one key area in a one- to two-hour practice session. This way, the golfer gives maximum attention to mastering the movement or sequence of movements he or she wants to improve. Practicing more than one or two items in one session leads to clutter and mental confusion.

Keep Your Playing Attitude Simple

It is a sound mental philosophy to go into a round with the simple goal of playing the way that you know you can play. This means that you choose to adopt an attitude that gives you the best chance to play to your physical and mental level for maximum enjoyment at any given moment on any given day. If you allow yourself to play the way that you know you can play, you are tapping into your natural and learned talent for success. Golfers often tell me that if they just focus on what they can control (themselves) and not worry about what they cannot control (other players in the group, other people's evaluations of them, scores, and so on) they play much more efficiently. By adopting this simple philosophy, you can play within yourself and accept your results. What usually happens when you create this simple playing attitude is that you start to relax and just go out and let it happen instead of trying hard to *make* something happen. When you do this, you are well on your way to tapping into your golfing potential.

Keep Your Preshot Routine Simple

Creating and using a preshot and preputt routine is systematically organizing your thoughts and behaviors into a procedure so that your physical movement is performed automatically. This means that you do not have to think about the separate components of the routine and address positions when you are actually going through those motions. By creating your routine via repetition and imprinting a neural blueprint in the brain, your mind is free to focus on the target while your body is engaged in performing movements that have been preprogrammed for motor execution. In order for this to occur, you must first identify which behaviors you will use and to what degree their function helps to create smoothness and focus in your routine. For the most part, I am not overly concerned with the number of steps that a player uses in establishing his or her customized preshot routine. However, the simpler you keep the process (understanding exactly why you are doing what you are doing at any moment during the routine), the easier it is to repeat.

Keep Your Swing Thoughts Simple

When people talk about great players keeping things simple, the name of Jack Nicklaus is often mentioned. Jack Nicklaus was known to have been a great proponent of using only one swing key or swing thought while he was hitting a golf shot. Choosing to attend to only one swing thought allowed Jack to concentrate fully on that key and to swing toward his target with trust and confidence. When players have more than one thought about their swing, their minds become flooded with too many instructions about how to hit the ball and their neural circuitry wires cross, creating chaos and confusion within the body's motor system. Therefore, it is vital that you step into the address position using only one swing key or thought and that you focus on that single item. This will allow you to swing freely without feeling the pangs of "paralysis by analysis."

Make a Clear and Simple Decision on the Shot at Hand

Once you start to assess and analyze what you are going to do with your golf shot, you should make a clear decision about what type of shot you are going to hit and then hit that decision. Golfers get into trouble when they step into the ball and their minds are not clear about what they really want to do with the shot. They often lack the clarity and commitment to hit the type of shot that they should play. What happens then is that they start to second-guess their initial decision, and while they stand over the ball they start to overanalyze and change their minds about what type of shot they are going to hit. The end result is usually an ineffective shot that results in disaster. It is crucial that you make a clear decision about what type of shot you want to hit and how you are going to hit it *before* you step into the address position. Remembering this simple maneuver will help create order and clarity with your golf shots.

Think This Simple Thought: Golf Is Play, Not Work

One of the hardest things to remember in the constant struggle for improvement is that golf is play, not work. Many golfers find themselves frustrated that long hours on the practice range make the game they love feel like hard manual labor. One young player recently said to me, "I started out loving this game, but in my quest to become club champion it has come to feel an awful lot like work." If this sounds similar to what you have been feeling, then it is absolutely vital to maintain the simple attitude that you love *playing* the game of golf. Remember, the main reason that you invest much of your free time into improving yourself is so that you can play better. First and foremost, golf is a game of play and enjoyment, and even the greatest touring professionals need to be reminded that they play their best golf when they create fun in their practice sessions and find ways to have fun during competition. (And this advice is for players whose vocation is golf and huge sums of money are at stake.) So don't take yourself too seriously. Making the game of golf an activity of enjoyment rather than a day of work and frustration tends to create lower scores and lower stress levels.

Summary

Keeping things simple, both on a physical and a mental level, is an important key to playing consistently well. Some of golf's greatest players have expounded on the virtues of keeping the game as simple as possible. Arnold Palmer once wrote in his classic book *Arnold Palmer: My Game and Yours* (page 12):

> We have been lured into too many complexities. We have forgotten that the game began with the very elemental discovery, by a Scotch shepherd who never had a lesson in his life, that he could knock a pebble an astounding distance with a good swift lick of his shepherd's crook, and that essentially the idea of the game

even today is simply to pick up a stick and a hit a ball with it, as straight and as hard as you can.

What Mr. Palmer was saying is that although the game of golf is very complex, the basic foundation of the game was, and still is, deceptively simple. It is up to each of us to find our own way to simplify the process. If we can keep things simple, we will find ways to create lower scores for ourselves and perhaps derive more enjoyment on the course. May all of your golf thoughts be simply wonderful.

Commandment 8

Thou Shalt Play with No Expectations

Expectations often get in our way. We have expectations about birthday or holiday gifts, raises or promotions, and even how our loved ones will greet us at the airport when we arrive after a flight. I'm not saying that expectations are all bad, because positive expectations do help to motivate people and create enthusiasm. But when results don't match expectations, people often end up feeling disappointed, sad, and frustrated.

For example, have you ever had anyone come up to you and say, "I have to tell you this joke—it's the funniest one I've ever heard," and then tell a joke that you don't find very funny at all? The person telling the joke raised your expectations. That is, the way the joke was presented ensured that *anything* that was said wouldn't have measured up to what you were imagining. You felt a bit "cheated" and disappointed from not enjoying this supposedly funny joke. This phenomenon also occurs on the golf course when expectations are prevalent in a golfer's mind.

When you golf with preconceived notions about how you are going to play or how you will score, you have a mental benchmark or standard that interferes with your natural talent and playing potential. The expectations take you out of the present moment and rob you of the ability to create flow and enjoy each moment and shot as the round progresses.

Golfers often become more concerned with achieving their expected standards than with what they need to do with the present shot. They become tense and disappointed if they feel they are not reaching their imagined measure of success. Playing an enjoyable round of golf becomes a day of work and frustration. With every unfulfilled expectation, frustration and disappointment set in and rob players of their confidence and composure. Let's examine a few of the expectation traps golfers frequently fall into.

Shooting a Certain Number or Score

When players have expectations of shooting a certain score, they often become "score conscious" and their attention is diverted from playing individual golf shots to merely counting. They turn their playing focus into a result or outcome orientation instead of a process or task orientation. They start to concentrate on *how many* shots they have taken in the round instead of focusing on doing their best with the shot at hand. Their self-talk says, *I'm already three over for the first four holes, so now I'm going to have to shoot par for the next five holes in order to beat my personal best of 39 for the front side.*

This creates tension and distorts focus, resulting in a tendency to take unnecessary gambles that lead to lost strokes. Then unmet expectations generate frustration and disappointment, which in turn may lead to self-doubt. If left unchecked, this turns into a negative performance cycle that can destroy what has taken many hours of practice and play to achieve.

This is a common issue for players who have trouble closing good rounds and instead throw away shots over the last couple of holes. For example, if a golfer is playing at par through the first fifteen holes and becomes aware of how she stands in relation to par, the focus now turns to expectations about score. If the expectation was to shoot par, the player will start to project what needs to be done in order to maintain par over the next three holes. The issue then becomes *Can I close the deal and bring this round home?* Rather than continuing with what has been working the entire day, the player reshifts her attention toward overall score and loses her present-shot focus.

What results from all of this is that the player is not just playing the shot at hand, but is burdened with all of the previous shots as a total collection of her efforts. The success of the day now hinges on how well the player can hit this shot and bring the total round home. This type of expectation thinking places a heavy psychological load on a golfer when trying to preserve a round. Preconceived expectations about score have ruined far more good rounds than can ever be counted. So put your expectations about score away and continue to give each shot total commitment and focus until the round for that day is completed. You give yourself a greater chance to play to your true potential if you can learn to do it this way.

Also, remember that the finish line is not just the end of your physical play. You do not have any score until you cross the finish line. This means that when you complete your physical tournament round, you have not completed your responsibility to yourself and your scorecard. In order to complete play, you must review your scorecard and your playing opponents' cards, and then review your card a second and perhaps a third time. When you feel that you have satisfied all of the necessary addition and other requirements, you can then sign your card and turn it in to the appropriate authority. Until you do all of these things, you have not finished your round.

Hitting the Golf Ball Perfectly

Expectations can interfere with your ball striking. Golfers who expect to hit the ball perfectly every time are positioning themselves for failure every time they play. If each shot they hit is not perfectly executed according to plan, then the entire golf day is essentially ruined and their enjoyment is nullified. An example of this is when golfers practice for weeks on the range to hit the ball a certain way (such as working the ball right to left) and then go to the course only to find that their shot pattern doesn't match what they have been working on. Of course, they become upset and frustrated. This may even happen when the ball flies to the target, but the result doesn't match or satisfy the golfer's preconceived expectation.

Golfers will continue to struggle in trying to "work" this shot into the day for every shot and force the issue until their round, composure, and score are ruined. This is a mental error that many golfers suffer through and never overcome. The sooner you can learn to cope effectively with the inconsistencies of your golf shots and swings, the sooner you will start to lower your scores. But in order to do this, you must be able to release your expectation of hitting shots perfectly and accept the results for what they are.

Even the great Ben Hogan, long remembered for his zeal for practice and for his shot-making efficiency, realized that his quest for perfection was a lonely man's vigil and that absolute perfection wasn't necessary to playing great golf. He once remarked that it wasn't until he gave up the notion of trying to swing with absolute perfection and just focused on playing the way he knew he could that he really started to win golf tournaments. The game is more fun when you place fewer demands on your performance and results. It is also easier on your psyche.

Positive Feelings and Thoughts

Positive expectations give you motivation and enthusiasm to prepare for an upcoming event, but once you step onto the golf course you need to let go of these expectations and get your mind into your target. This must become habitual. If you wonder how positive expectations could be bad or unproductive, let me ask you a question. Have you ever had a day when you went to the golf course with positive expectations but your performance was lackluster? If you responded yes, you're certainly not alone. This is because performance is a "present" activity.

Positive expectations alone do not ensure success. What you need is a performance mindset that absorbs target information coupled with a routine that is automatic and allows you to play and respond appropriately to your target. Positive expectations are good for developing confidence before you play, but when you arrive at the golf course, leave all expectations, good or bad, at the clubhouse gate. You will be much better off playing with a mind that is into your target in the present moment than having expectations of what could be or should be. By eliminating the expectations you remove the shackles from your mind and release yourself from accountability to any preset standards of performance, freeing your mind and body to play to your true potential.

Mind Stuff: Things to Do to Play Great
What Should I Expect While Playing?

Now that you know how expectations can affect your performance, you're probably wondering what you should expect while getting ready to play or when you are in the middle of your round. Here are a few tactics that may help.

Expect the Best but Be Prepared for the Worst

You must prepare your mind and body to do the very best you can on each shot and believe that you can handle anything that comes along. The great Walter Hagen once said, "Whatever happens on the golf course is OK, because if I put the ball in trouble I know I have the skills to get it out of trouble and back into play." I think this is a great way to think because it provides you, the performer, with an attitude that gives you self-control, no matter what the results or circumstances. This philosophy worked quite well for Walter, and it can also work for you.

Make a Total Commitment

Develop the philosophy that the only thing you expect of yourself while playing is that on every shot you make the commitment to really get into your target, to swing with trust, and finally to accept the result and move on to the next shot with the same expectation of commitment. This may be the only expectation that truly works for shooting low scores and playing to your potential on the golf course. It provides you with the creative license and freedom to swing with trust on every shot. It also allows you the ability to accept what you cannot control. Playing golf with the only expectation that you are giving every shot your total effort and commitment and accepting the result is the best way to start playing to your true potential.

Expect the Unexpected

Expecting the unexpected is a strategy that can help you not become so upset or deflated when things go askew. Learn to remain patient and realize that the inconsistencies and unexpected ironies of the day's play are part of what makes golf so great. Knowing that unexpected events, bounces, and shots can and will happen during a round of golf makes the game interesting and fun. Think about it: if every round of golf were vanilla and bland, would you find it as intoxicating and exciting as you do now? I don't think so. One of the most exciting features of playing golf is that you never know what to expect at the next hole, the next dogleg, the next putt. The mystery of not really knowing what will happen is what keeps bringing you back for more.

Summary

Expectations get in the way of optimal performance because they set a preconceived measure of success that you must match or exceed every time you tee it up. If you have lofty expectations about what you want to do in a round or about a certain number to shoot, you will lose focus on playing one shot at a time and staying in the present moment. What eventually results from failing to meet the demands of your expectations is disappointment, frustration, and anger, which ruin your ability to stay motivated and focused for the duration of the round. The sooner you can forget about what or how you "should be" scoring and swinging and start focusing on the task at hand, the sooner things will fall into place and positive outcomes will happen as a result of playing versus expecting.

So relax and leave your expectations outside the clubhouse gates. *Do* get into your targets and fire away with confidence and trust. The sooner you can eliminate the burden of unfulfilled expectations, the sooner you will play to your true potential. May you always play with childlike freedom without the burden of self-imposed expectations.

Thou Shalt Play with Trust

Trust. It's the buzzword of this decade. It seems that you hear and read about trust every day. You hear about it on your radio as you drive to work, you see it on TV, and you even hear your favorite golf professionals mutter to themselves that they didn't trust their swings when they hit bad shots. Little wonder, then, that the word *trust* has found its way into golf's vocabulary and into your golf thoughts. Trust is a big deal because everything you do in golf (as in life) is based on it.

You may wonder why I consider trust of paramount importance to your golf game. It is because the level of trust that you have of yourself and of your golf game is a reflection of how you think, feel, and behave about certain golf situations. Consider the following three questions and answer them as honestly as you can about your ability to trust while playing golf:

1. Do you find when you are about to play in a big tournament or match that you worry you won't be able to play your normal game?
2. Have you ever been over an important shot and discovered that you weren't sure of your ability to execute the shot correctly?

3. Have you ever been over a shot and instinctively known that although you are trying your best, the shot will still turn out poorly?

If you answered yes to any of these questions, it is likely that you lacked trust in your ability at that single moment and felt out of control. This feeling of being out of control and lacking trust is normal for many golfers. Sometimes they trust themselves, and other times they don't. Most golfers would like to be able to trust themselves all the time. First, it is important to understand exactly what trust is in golf terms and to acquire a way to build trust so that we can be more trusting in any golf situation that we encounter. Let's take a closer look at this issue.

Golf and Trust: The Results Are Black and White

Trust is categorical in nature: you either trust your golfing ability, your judgment, and your decision making, or you don't. It's really quite simple. Either you trust yourself totally or you don't trust yourself at all. It's black and white. There is no "gray" area in the land of trust, especially on the golf course.

Playing golf with a high level of trust means performing without doubt and the fearful expectation that something bad will happen. It also means that you can swing to your target without having to overcontrol yourself trying to hit the ball just right. When you play with trust you give yourself the confidence that everything will be all right. In a sense, it means that you can play without fear and without hindering thoughts of self-doubt and worry.

Let's examine the definition of the word *trust*. Merriam-Webster's dictionary uses these keys to define trust:

> assured reliance on the character, strength, or truth of someone or something; one in which confidence is placed; confident hope; care, custody, dependence, and faith in someone or something

These definitions suggest that when you place an assured reliance that someone or something will come through for you, you gain confidence and hope from that placement of trust. In golf, when you place trust in yourself, you are placing an assured reliance that *you* will come through for *you*. This reliance manifests itself in your analysis of the situation, your decision about what type of shot to hit, and in the execution of each swing.

Trust: Golf Swing and Golf Play Definitions

Another way to view trust is in terms of golf swing mechanics. In the arena of motor learning, trust means that you let go of conscious overcontrolling tendencies and allow automatic processes that you have learned via practice to come forth. In simpler terms, when you trust, you allow your golfing talent to come through without having to consciously think about your swing mechanics. That's why you practice: to learn the proper sequence of movements so that the sequence becomes a habit.

When you consciously try to swing the golf club perfectly, you coerce the motion instead of allowing the swing to occur fluidly and automatically. In effect, if you don't allow yourself to trust while swinging the golf club you negate all the time and effort you spent practicing.

Think about this: if you don't trust your ability when you're swinging a five-iron at a pin that is tucked behind some trouble, what are you trusting? Are you trusting the ball's intelligence to find the target on its own? It's funny, but a lot of golfers do just that. They misplace their trust (or fail to trust) and flail at the ball without any notion of what may happen. The result is that their golfing expectations are once again not met. This lack of trust in one's golf ability and judgment makes the game extremely difficult and, many times, unfulfilling.

Perhaps the main reason trust is so difficult to obtain is that it requires great amounts of self-discipline and time to develop. This may be why trust is such a precious commodity in our society as well. Consider, for a moment, your closest friends. How long did it take before you could trust them? Have you ever heard of anyone involved in a romantic relationship who asked their partner, "Don't you trust me?" It could be the reason that question is asked is many people do not have the capability to trust because they don't even trust themselves.

Without the ability to trust yourself, how can you ever place your trust in anyone or anything else? In the sport of golf, you *must* trust yourself, because wherever you go in this game and at whatever level you play, you're alone with nothing but your thoughts and beliefs about your ability. Thus it is vital to your golfing potential that you learn to trust your mind, your feelings, and your golfing instinct.

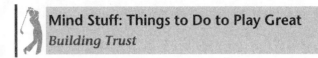

Building and enhancing trust is a lifelong process. Commit to these suggestions and notice how your scores and attitude improve.

Make a Clear Decision About Your Shot and Commit to It

When you are analyzing and deciding on what type of shot to hit, listen to your inner voice. It will guide you to make the right decision at that particular moment. Often when Tour players are undecided about whether to chip with a wedge or use a less-lofted club (or even putt) they will listen to their inner voice to make a clear and prudent decision. This decision will be based on how confident they feel about a certain club or shot, or what type of shot is most likely to achieve the best result at that particular moment. You should try to emulate this thinking. By using your inner voice to help guide your thoughts, you give yourself the psychological freedom to know that you have made the right decision. Knowing that you have made a clear decision will help you be specific about what you want to do with the shot and keep your swing motion fluid under pressure.

Walter Hagen was once credited as saying, "I would rather be of clear mind and decision with the wrong club than with an unclear mind and the right club." This type of thinking allowed Walter to swing freely, knowing that he made the right choice of club and shot. This type of thinking is a key foundation for building trust. Being decisive about what type of shot you want to make and committing to that feeling will transfer to more confident swings when you are faced with high-pressure situations.

When Preparing to Swing, Use a Trust Cue

You might find it helpful when getting ready to swing the club to organize a number of your thoughts into one priority cue designed to help you focus on one important aspect of your swing. It may be a feeling, a word, or a phrase. Whatever it is, make it your *trust cue*. That is, if you feel that you want to swing with a fuller turn, think "big turn" and concentrate on that feeling. The cue prompts you to focus on turning your shoulders and body for a full windup. Using a trust cue allows you to focus on one aspect that will aid in getting the ball where you want it to go. For years, Jack Nicklaus talked about using one or two swing keys, and he had great success with this tactic. You can do the same thing mentally and emotionally when you use a trust cue. Although a trust cue doesn't have to be a swing key, it is used to give you a "do this" mentality versus focusing on "what if."

Remember John Daly's cue word in the 1991 PGA Championship? John used the word "kill" every time he hit his driver at the long Crooked Stick Golf Course in Carmel, Indiana. John used his cue word to overpower "the Stick" and hit his driver with accuracy and awesome length to eventually win the PGA Championship. It worked for John, and I know that it can work for you. The key is to find a trust cue that is simple to use and that allows you to focus on process instead of results or outcomes.

Focus on Where You Want the Ball to Go
and Then Let It Go

When you hear great golfers and golf teachers say, "free it up and let it go," they are usually talking about letting go of all the tension that comes from trying to hit the golf ball perfectly. The secret is that you gain more control by letting go of trying to control. When you allow yourself to swing freely instead of trying to control, your body performs more efficiently. Have you ever seen a golfer hit her second ball straight down the center of the fairway after hitting her first ball out of bounds? After the disappointment of the initial bad shot, what usually happens next is that the golfer pulls out a second ball, looks at where she wants to hit the ball, and just swings, sending the second ball straight down the middle of the fairway. She might wonder, *Why didn't I do that the first time?* The reason is that she didn't allow herself to fully trust and let her swing occur automatically. This automatic mode occurs most frequently when golfers are not consciously thinking about how to strike the ball, but rather where to hit it (the target), without conscious interference.

So when you practice on the range, focus on a particular target, focus your mind and body on where you want the ball to go, and then swing away. Enjoy the feeling of swinging versus controlling and see if you notice the difference. This is a vital point if you want to develop trust in your game. Also, allow yourself a number of rounds to play without keeping score or tracking fulfilled or unfulfilled expectations. Focusing on just hitting the ball to your target (without keeping score) will give you a greater appreciation of playing free without the burden of playing to some standard.

Take Your Time

Trusting is easy when things are going well. In fact, when you are playing good golf, trust is a nonissue. When you really trust, you don't even have to think about it. It feels as if you are playing but not really "trying" to play, and your mind is quiet. In the same way, when people truly trust each other in a loving relationship the word *trust* rarely comes up, because trust between them is implicit. If you are playing golf and you totally trust your instinct and your golfing talent, you don't give yourself a chance to doubt or mistrust. Thus, doubt doesn't enter your thought process or get into your head. However, when you doubt your ability and your decision making, you may want to take control and in turn overcontrol. This leads you to "try" instead of "do."

As in relationships, the development of trust in golf takes time. Give yourself every opportunity to build trust in your game, knowing that trust is the most difficult aspect of golf (and in life, some might argue) to permanently attain. Thus it becomes a constant life and golf improvement goal. Touring professionals who have attained their personal goals have had to learn to trust what was best for them and to live and die by that trust. It is one virtue that is well worth the sacrifice.

Summary

In our everyday lives, if we cannot trust we cannot move. Without trust, we would live our lives in constant fear. Imagine not trusting the pilot who flies the plane you are traveling on. How about not trusting the bus driver or cab driver who controls the vehicle you're riding in? Trust is an important component of our golfing life, too. Golfers who do not trust themselves or their ability to swing the club correctly will always play with a high level of anxiety and doubt. Without the ability to trust your choices and your talent, you are finished even before you hit your ball off the opening tee.

Think of a round of golf when you played your very best. Did it seem easy? Did you feel that the shots were simple to execute and that you made good decisions and had the capacity to execute those decisions? If you answered yes, then you have achieved trust on the golf course. Trust is total confidence in yourself and your abilities. It is so important to train your body and mind to trust, but it isn't easy. Nothing worthwhile ever is. Without trust, golf is a game of conscious trying and coercion, rather than an enjoyable experience where everything is going to be OK, no matter what you score. Trust is a belief that *you* will come through for *you*. As you learn to create and play with trust, you will find that it becomes a nonissue, which will in turn produce greater trust. May you always believe in yourself and trust your talent.

Thou Shalt Never, Ever Give Up

This final chapter covers what may be the most important component of your performance in golf and life. That is why I have saved it until last. This tenth commandment is about the virtue of persistence, of never giving up. It is about staying the course until you ultimately succeed. It is about the power of your spirit and a sacred trust that each of us has with our true self: to never give up on ourselves, our aspirations, our dreams. It is also about refusing to give in to trying circumstances, about hanging in there when reason tells you that the competition is over and that you are done for the day. It is about refusing to tank or to loaf through a round of golf and staying focused on making every shot count, no matter what your running total is or how your day has been going.

Never giving up is about you giving yourself the very best effort you can toward being successful, no matter how unsuccessful you have been throughout the day, the week, or the year. It also is about learning from your failings and moving forward toward success. Never giving up is a mental, emotional, and volitional attribute that every warrior athlete under-

89

stands. It is a virtue of every golf champion who has ever walked on a course, whether at your local golf club or on the PGA and LPGA Tours. It is a personal resolve that every golfer needs to tap into during times of trouble and uncertainty. Never giving up turns an average competitor into a worthy foe who is hard to beat. It is an attribute that is worth your weight in gold.

"Never Give In" and the Battle of Britain

"Never give in, never give in, never, never, never, never." This saying has historical significance because of the simplicity of its meaning. I use this famous quote by Sir Winston Churchill because of the gravity of the situation at the moment in which he relayed the message to the British citizens during the Battle of Britain in 1941. Sir Winston Churchill's radio message provided motivation and inspiration to the English people, who were suffering months of relentless aerial bombing attacks by the German Luftwaffe.

In their burning homes and bomb shelters, the people of Great Britain, inspired by Churchill's fighting spirit, dug in and refused to give up. Continued German bombardment only solidified the British spirit into a steely resolve. The English people persevered and fought back and outlasted the German war machine that had them severely outnumbered. Their determination turned the tide of certain defeat into a war-changing victory. The efforts of the people of Great Britain were a testament to the value of words. Sir Winston Churchill paid homage to the moral fortitude of his people when he uttered the famous words, "Never in the field of human conflicts was so much owed by so many to so few." The Battle of Britain is a historical reminder of the power of the human spirit that knows no boundaries when overwhelming challenges present themselves.

Volition, Willpower, and the Human Spirit

As a human being, you have a sense of determination to see something through to its completion. You have *volition*, the power to use your will to see something through and to stand firm in your decisions. Volition involves using your personal willpower to overcome obstacles and impediments. The function of free will and personal choice was studied in depth by the father of modern psychology, William James, who once stated that "the greatest discovery of my generation is that a human being can alter his life by altering his attitudes of mind."

This statement suggests that as human beings we can change our lives by simply changing our attitudes and our purposeful behaviors and by altering how we perceive and believe things to be. This is why in the heat of battles and waging wars, propaganda and slander play an important role: specifically, to disrupt and break the spirit and purposeful intent of the competing side. Propaganda creates doubt and confusion about the target's philosophy and free will. The primary objective in propaganda is to create psychological and emotional havoc, kill hope, and sabotage human spirit. When an opponent in war or sports loses hope and their determined spirit is broken, victory for the opposing side is imminent.

This is why it is so important to stay motivated to succeed and to never give up or admit defeat. This recurring theme throughout history has made the difference between victory and defeat, freedom and bondage, life and death. As in the Battle of Britain and in every war that has ever been staged, one never knows when the tide will turn in one's favor and generate positive momentum. That is why you must never, ever give in. Giving in, throwing in the towel, or admitting failure and defeat before the contest is completely decided is psychological surrender that often leads to emotional devastation soon after. This same phenomenon happens on the golf course as well.

The Value of Never Giving Up in Golf

The notion of never giving up may sound trite, but every great golfer has understood the value of persistence in golf. In fact, I believe that the greatest golfers of every decade have known this right from the very start of their careers. But don't think that this sentiment applies only to the top professionals. This message holds true for you and your golf partners as well. Of the golfers you play with day in and day out, the ones who score consistently well have the same persistence and determination in their golf games that the best players on Tour have. They know that their greatest asset in their pursuit of top-level performance is their dogged determination to do their best and the competitive spirit of an athletic warrior.

It is no coincidence that the greatest champions of every sport know the importance of total dedication to their sport and commit every day to 100 percent effort, regardless of results. But, more important, they value staying committed to their philosophies and dreams. Giving up on their dreams and throwing in the towel during a poor performance is simply unacceptable to them. One great example of a player who models these qualities is Sweden's Annika Sorenstam.

Annika Sorenstam and the Will to Win

Annika Sorenstam is a champion and a mentally and emotionally tough competitor. A great deal of her winning is attributed to her outstanding ball-striking ability, but a significant competitive edge she has is a personal resolve to persevere and to dig deep within herself to do whatever it takes to win. Consider her winning performances in 2002. She won eleven titles on the LPGA Tour and two other world titles for a total of thirteen victories in one season. That total broke existing records from 1968 held by Hall of Famers Kathy Whitworth and Carol Mann. When asked how she felt about winning her record-tying tenth victory, Sorenstam responded, "I told my caddie today that I am in the position that I want to be in. That this is what I have been waiting for, to win my tenth victory. I said that I am going to do everything that I can do today and that nothing is going to stop me."

Sorenstam's statement teaches us several key components of mental and emotional hardiness that you can emulate in your game. First, she reflected with her caddie that she loved the position that she put herself in by virtue of her good play. She enjoyed being in contention to win the tournament. Second, Sorenstam was looking forward to the challenge of performing prior to the actual competition. These are prime examples of a performer's mindset. She loved both the pressure and the chance to display her talent. Third, she told herself that she was going to do whatever it took to give herself every opportunity to succeed. This is a purposeful statement of intention and commitment.

Finally, she made the ultimate statement of human willpower, "Nothing is going to stop me." Little wonder that Annika Sorenstam went on in 2002 and 2003 to dominate the golfing world and enter the World Golf Hall of Fame. Her competitiveness and persistence are qualities every golfer should strive to emulate.

Annika Sorenstam realized that if she kept thinking and doing the same good things shot after shot, round after round, she would build a platform for success down the road. Remember, all it takes to get a round going is to hang in there and hit one good shot. Great golfers continually tell me that when things are going poorly, the best thing that they do for their golf games is to hang in there, stay mentally tough, and stay focused on the shot at hand. Doing these things allows them the greatest chance of developing patience, composure, and a strong mental attitude that reinforces the notion of never, ever giving in. This philosophy has worked well for Annika and can do the same for you.

Tiger Woods and the 1997 Masters

Another great example of a golfer staying focused and not giving up during a tournament was Tiger Woods during the 1997

Masters at Augusta, Georgia. Tiger was walking up the eighteenth fairway with a twelve-shot advantage and anticipating a record-breaking finish. For all practical purposes, he could have been fitted for his first green jacket in the middle of the fairway. Many golfers would have been satisfied to simply play out the string (or go through the motions on the last series of shots) and to just finish and move on to the winner's circle. But more was at stake than just winning the tournament and the scoring record at Augusta. I'm talking about the volitional characteristic of always finishing what you have started with full intent and purposefulness, not giving up until your task is *done*.

Tiger went on to say after the awards ceremony that as he was walking up the fairway, his mind was starting to wander and jump into the future. He was thinking of all the things he had done his whole life to prepare for this moment. He was starting to think about how his mother and father would be proud of him and how his life would be changed by winning a major championship. Imagine how hard it would be to dismiss these types of thoughts when all you have to do is make contact with the golf ball in order to realize your wildest dreams.

But Tiger shook himself into the present moment and reminded himself internally to "finish the race." He went on to say that his words inside his head were: *Tiger, come on now, you've still got work to do. This round and golf tournament are not over. Hang in there and finish your race. Finish the race.* Tiger went on to get up and down for his par on the eighteenth hole, and the rest is history.

The lesson of this story is that you should never give up your golfing "race" until the last putt is completed. A round of golf is never over until you have signed your scorecard and given each shot full intention and commitment. Staying focused and never giving anything but your best effort on every shot throughout your golfing round will help you develop into a mentally tough and emotionally resilient golfer.

Mind Stuff: Things to Do to Play Great
Creating a Mentally Tough Mindset

Giving your best effort on every shot and staying the course are golden rules to great golf. The following strategies will help you become mentally and emotionally tough.

Commit Yourself to a Personal Philosophy that Suggests You Love to Compete

It is important to adopt an attitude that you love to compete and to put your game on the line. Don't be afraid to show the world (or yourself) what you can do, because many people are better golfers than they give themselves credit for being. They tend to underestimate their playing ability when they go into competitions. Many golfers who come to me for help undermine their own talent and sabotage their own success. Don't fall into this negative trap. Give yourself credit. Don't sell yourself short. Strive to become an athletic warrior and keep reminding yourself that you love to compete. Remember that you are here to play your game and that nothing else or no one else really matters. This day is about *your* striving to be excellent for *yourself*.

Knowing that you have prepared your mind and body to perform well on any given day helps you to promote a playing philosophy that you play your game and that you can play anywhere, with anyone, at any time, under any conditions. The bottom line is this: no one else really cares about your game or about how you play. So get over your self-doubt, release the thought of how others may view you, and move forward to becoming the toughest competitor you can be. Play for the most important person in the world: you.

Use Positive Self-Talk to Motivate and Inspire

As the old saying goes, "When the going gets tough, the tough get going." Golfers who are mentally tough are always finding ways to keep their spirits up and to create and sustain positive golf momentum. One of the best things you can do for yourself when the tough times come on the golf course (and believe me, they will come) is to give yourself a pep talk. It is a good strategy to keep yourself moving in a positive direction and to start every shot with renewed interest and vigor, especially when you are having a poor day. It is so important that your self-talk and thoughts are invigorated with purposefulness and hope, because once the enthusiasm and hope are gone you will be finished emotionally for the day and it will become impossible to persist.

Give yourself a key word or a key phrase such as "Hang in there" or "Let's get this one" and don't let yourself think negative thoughts of tanking, giving in, or letting up. I tell my golfers to write a motivational phrase inside their cap lining like "Believe in yourself" or "Stay on task." Many of my players have been surprised at how a small thing like taking off their hat and looking down into the bill to see their mental reminder has given them new life in the middle of the round. The next time

you are a bit depressed on the course, take the time to give
yourself a pep talk and remind yourself that you have what it
takes and that you are a tough competitor who never gives up.

Give 100 Percent Effort in Every Practice Session

Golf champions love to compete and display their talent in
tournament competitions. That is why they are champions.
However, champions are not created on the day of the tournament; they are created on the practice greens and driving ranges
of the world. Long before a championship is ever won by a
golfer, that player has put in hundreds, perhaps thousands, of
hours practicing and becoming comfortable with his or her
playing style and golfing technique. By trusting their training
regimen and believing in themselves and their work ethic, golfers can play to their earned talent level in a tournament. Champions are not born but made, one practice shot at a time.

The quality of your practice is always going to show up in
the quality of your performance. Every great athlete knows this
to be true. That is why you want to give 100 percent effort on
every shot in your practices—because you are setting a psychological and emotional standard of performance within your
mind and body. It is a personal excellence quality that you create for yourself every day. In a very real sense, you are creating
a habit that will show up in competition.

Give 100 Percent Effort in Every Playing Round

Just as important as practicing with 100 percent effort is *playing* with 100 percent effort. This means that no matter how you
score or strike the ball, you will give every shot your ultimate
best. For example, imagine that you are on the seventeenth

green and you haven't made a putt all day. Rather than dwelling on how badly you have been putting, you are singularly devoted to making this particular putt because it is all you can control at this moment. It doesn't matter what has happened before or what this putt represents on the scorecard. All you have is this moment and this putt. You are in the now.

Summary

Never giving up during a golf round is a continuous process. Every single shot is a special moment in your golfing life to execute as efficiently as you can. Each day on the links your thinking, shot-making ability, and emotional resolve will be tested. Within your mind, always give 100 percent effort. Do not allow give-up or let-up. This is the ultimate mental habit that you create for yourself. It is the foundation for golfing excellence from which you draw strength and emotional fortitude. The results of this resolve will be the greatest gift you will ever give yourself.

The Ten Commandments of Mindpower Golf

1. **Thou shalt have a great attitude.** Great golf always begins and ends with a player creating and maintaining a great attitude. A positive attitude is the ultimate emotional fuel for optimal golf performance.
2. **Thou shalt always believe in thyself.** Believing in yourself is fundamental to building trust and self-confidence. Know that you have the skills to handle whatever happens on the golf course.
3. **Thou shalt play thine own game.** Playing your own game is playing to your ability level. Understand how you play, and execute your shot according to your personal playing style.
4. **Thou shalt play one shot at a time.** Playing one shot at a time is staying focused in the moment and putting your absolute best effort into that single moment. Stay in the now.
5. **Thou shalt play with patience.** Playing with patience and composure ensures that you will play with an emotional balance. It helps you to maintain a good rhythm

and adhere to your desired playing strategy. Playing with patience helps you to stay in the present moment and concentrate fully on the shot at hand.

6. **Thou shalt commit to every shot.** Commitment to every shot gives you a chance to execute every shot with full intent and purposefulness. It also helps you implement positive action into every moment and eliminate negative anxiety.

7. **Thou shalt keep thy game simple.** The simplicity of your thoughts and specificity of your golf intentions lead to greater swing efficiency and more consistent scoring.

8. **Thou shalt play with no expectations.** Expectations are preset standards that interfere with simply playing your game. The only expectation that works in a performance setting is the expectation to be totally focused in the moment and strive to stay on task in that moment.

9. **Thou shalt play with trust.** Trust is the conscious letting go of overcontrolling tendencies to hit the ball correctly. When you play with trust, you allow yourself to swing to the target and forget worrying about how to swing. Playing with trust is about letting go of trying hard and just playing golf.

10. **Thou shalt never, ever give up.** Never giving up is about having emotional and mental resolve that suggests you won't quit or give in. You will give your best on each shot until the very end. This value is fundamental to success.

Index

Adjustment, attitude, 2–5
Anger, swinging away, 49
Arnold Palmer: My Game and Yours (Palmer), 68–69
Assess shot, 39–40
Attitude, 1–12
  about, 1–2
  adjustment, 2–5
  case study, 2–5
  defined, 10–11
  emotions and, 5–6
  simplified game strategy, 65
Attitude strategies, 6–11
  attitude championship, 8–9
  define great attitude, 10–11
  "I Can Handle It" attitude, 7–8
  imitate players with great attitude, 10
  pep talks, 9–10

Ball striking, expectations, 74–75

Case study, attitude, 2–5
Churchill, Winston, 90
Commandments
  about, xii
  short version, 101–2

Commitment, 51–59
  about, 51–52
  to chosen shot, 39, 40
  golfing self, 52
  strategies, 55–59
  veteran golfer, 52–53
Commitment strategies
  golf goals, 55–56
  practice schedule, 56–57
  preshot routine, 57–58
  target, 58–59
Competition, persistence strategies, 96–97
Composure, 11
Confidence, xiii, 47

Daly, John, 84
David Leadbetter World Teaching Headquarters, x
Distractions, strategies for, 31–32
Dyer, Wayne, 27

Effort, xviii, 98–99
Ego-protecting behavior, 2–4
Els, Ernie, 12
Emotionally challenged golfers, xiii

Emotions
  attitude and, 5–6
  golf and, xi–xii
Expectations, 71–78
  about, 71–72
  ball striking, 74–75
  positive feelings and thoughts,
    75–76
  scores, 72–74
  strategies, 76–77

Fasth, Niclas, 19
Flick, Jim, 8
Focus on ball, strategies for, 85
Fulke, Pierre, 19

Goals, simplified game strategies
    for, 64
Golf characteristics, your, 27–28
Golfing self, 52

Hagen, Walter, 76, 84
Harmon, Butch, 16
Hitting
  play your game, 28–29
  staying in the moment, 39, 40
Hogan, Ben, xi, 14
Howell, Charles III, 12

"I Can Handle It" attitude
    strategy, 7–8
Imitate players with great
    attitude strategy, 10
Improvement through self-belief,
    16–17

James, William, 91–92
Jim Flick on Golf (Flick), 8

Kite, Tom, 29–30
Knowing, self-belief, 14–16

Langer, Bernhard, 19
Leadbetter, David, x, xiii
The Little Engine That Could, 23

McGinley, Paul, 19
McGraw, Phil, 1
Mental game of golf, ix–x
Mickelson, Phil, 18–20
Montgomerie, Colin, 19

Nicklaus, Jack, 14, 43, 84

One-shot mindset, 35–42
  about, 35
  defined, 36–37
  focus on the moment,
    37–41
  staying in the moment
    exercise, 35–36

Palmer, Arnold, 14, 68–69
Patience, 11, 43–50
  about, 43
  confidence and, 47
  statistics, 43–44
  strategies, 48–49
  Woods, Tiger, 45–47
Pep talk strategy, 9–10
Persistence, 89–99
  about, 89–90
  Sorenstam, Annika, 93–94
  value, 92–93
  volition, 91–92
  willpower, 91–92
  Woods, Tiger, 94–96

Persistence strategies, 96–99
  competition, 96–97
  effort, 98–99
  positive self-talk, 97–98
  practice sessions, 98
Play your game, 25–33
  about, 25–33
  hit the right shot, 28–29
  Kite, Tom, 29–30
  you are the game, 26–27
  your golf characteristics,
    27–28
  at your speed, 30–31
Positive feelings and thoughts,
  expectations for, 75–76
Positive reinforcement strategy,
  48–49
Positive self-talk, 49–50, 97–98
Practice sessions
  persistence strategy, 98
  simplified game strategy,
    64–65
Preshot routine, 65–66
Price, Phillip, 19–20

Responsibility, self-belief and,
  17–18
Ryder Cup, 18–20

Sam Snead Teaches You His
  Simple Key Approach to Golf
  (Snead), 61
Scores, expectations and,
  72–74
Self-belief, 13–23
  about, 13–14
  knowing, 14–16
  responsibility, 17–18

Ryder Cup, 18–20
  Woods, Tiger, 16–17
Self-doubt, xviii
Self-improvement strategy,
  20–22
Self-talk, 21, 49–50
Shot commitment strategy,
  83–84
Shots, assess, 39–40
Simplified game, 61–69
  about, 61–62
  paper clip analogy, 63
Simplified game strategies,
  63–68
  goals, 64
  playing attitude, 65
  practice sessions, 64–65
  preshot routine, 65–66
  swing thoughts, 66–67
Snead, Sam, 14, 61
Sorenstam, Annika, 14, 93–94
Speed, of play, 30–31
Staying in the moment
  accept result, 39, 41
  assess shot, 39–40
  commit to chosen shot, 39, 40
  hit the ball, 39, 40
  one-shot mindset, 35–36
Strategies
  attitude, 6–11
  build commitment, 55–59
  distractions, 31–32
  expectations, 76–77
  one-shot mindset, 41
  patience, 48–49
  persistence, 96–99
  positive reinforcement, 48–49
  self-improvement, 20–22

simplified game,
    63–68
  trust, 83–86
Swings
  anger away, 49
  thoughts, 66–67
  trust, 81–82
  trust strategies, 84

Teske, Rachel, 14
Time, trust strategy and, 86
Torrance, Sam, 18
Trust, 79–87
  about, 79–80
  defined, 80–81
  golf swing mechanics,
      81–82

Trust strategies, 83–86
  focus on ball, 85
  shot commitment, 83–84
  swing, 84
  time, 86

Value, of persistence, 92–93
Volition, 91–92

Willpower, 91–92
Winters, Robert, x
Woods, Tiger, xvii, 12, 14
  patience, 45–47
  persistence, 94–96
  self-belief, 16–17

You are the game, 26–27